The FJH Classic Scale Book

**MAJOR AND MINOR SCALES, CHORDS, CADENCES, AND ARPEGGIOS
WITH INSTRUCTIONAL MATERIAL AND PRACTICE GUIDES**

by Victoria McArthur & Edwin McLean

CONTENTS

Understanding Major Scales

HALF STEPS AND WHOLE STEPS

A **half step (H)** is the closest key to the right or left of any key.

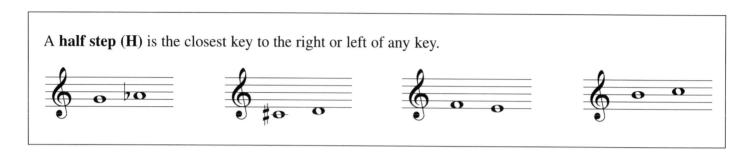

A **whole step (W)** is made up of two half steps.

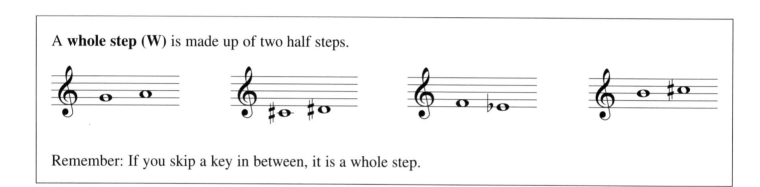

Remember: If you skip a key in between, it is a whole step.

THE MAJOR SCALE

Every major scale is built from half steps and whole steps in this order:

W W H W W W H

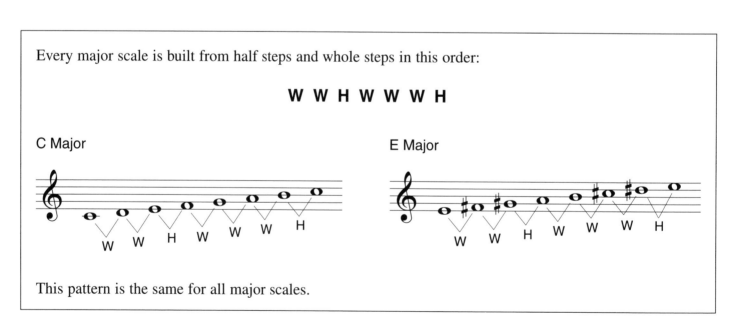

This pattern is the same for all major scales.

Understanding Minor Scales

MINOR SCALES

Minor scales use the same key signature as their related major scale. For instance, A minor is the relative minor of C major, and uses the same key signature of no sharps or flats.

Natural Minor

The natural minor scale is built by using the notes of the major scale beginning with the sixth note (degree) of the scale.

C Major

A Natural Minor

A minor scale built from a major scale in this way is called *natural* minor because no accidentals are used.

Harmonic Minor

The harmonic minor scale is built by raising the **seventh** note (degree) of the natural minor scale one half step.

A Harmonic Minor

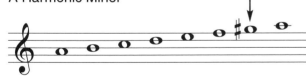

Melodic Minor

The melodic minor scale is built by raising by one half step both the **sixth** and **seventh** notes (degrees) of the natural minor scale when ascending (going up), then lowering them when descending (going down).

A Melodic Minor

Checklist for Scales

MAJOR SCALES

QUARTERS IN PARALLEL MOTION, 1 OCTAVE

	C	G	D	A	E	B	F#	F	Bb	Eb	Ab	Db	Gb
♩ = 60													
♩ = 96													
♩ = 144													
♩ =													

EIGHTHS IN PARALLEL MOTION, 2 OCTAVES

	C	G	D	A	E	B	F#	F	Bb	Eb	Ab	Db	Gb
♩ = 52													
♩ = 84													
♩ = 120													
♩ =													

CONTRARY MOTION

	C	G	D	A	E	B	F#	F	Bb	Eb	Ab	Db	Gb
♩ = 52													
♩ = 84													
♩ = 120													
♩ =													

THIRDS

	C	G	D	A	E	B	F#	F	Bb	Eb	Ab	Db	Gb
♩ = 52													
♩ = 84													
♩ = 120													
♩ =													

SIXTHS

	C	G	D	A	E	B	F#	F	Bb	Eb	Ab	Db	Gb
♩ = 52													
♩ = 84													
♩ = 120													
♩ =													

MINOR SCALES

NATURAL MINOR, QUARTERS IN PARALLEL MOTION, 1 OCTAVE

	a	e	b	f#	c#	g#	d#	d	g	c	f	bb	eb
♩ = 60													
♩ = 96													
♩ = 144													
♩ =													

NATURAL MINOR, EIGHTHS IN PARALLEL MOTION, 2 OCTAVES

	a	e	b	f#	c#	g#	d#	d	g	c	f	bb	eb
♩ = 52													
♩ = 84													
♩ = 120													
♩ =													

HARMONIC MINOR, EIGHTHS IN PARALLEL MOTION

	a	e	b	f#	c#	g#	d#	d	g	c	f	bb	eb
♩ = 52													
♩ = 84													
♩ = 120													
♩ =													

HARMONIC MINOR, CONTRARY MOTION

	a	e	b	f#	c#	g#	d#	d	g	c	f	bb	eb
♩ = 52													
♩ = 84													
♩ = 120													
♩ =													

MELODIC MINOR, PARALLEL MOTION

	a	e	b	f#	c#	g#	d#	d	g	c	f	bb	eb
♩ = 52													
♩ = 84													
♩ = 120													
♩ =													

Checklist for Triads, Arpeggios, and Cadences

MAJOR

MAJOR TRIADS AND INVERSIONS, BLOCK

	C	G	D	A	E	B	F♯	F	B♭	E♭	A♭	D♭	G♭
♩ = 48													
♩ = 66													
♩ = 92													
♩ =													

MAJOR TRIADS AND INVERSIONS, BROKEN

	C	G	D	A	E	B	F♯	F	B♭	E♭	A♭	D♭	G♭
♩. = 40													
♩. = 72													
♩. = 104													
♩. =													

MAJOR ARPEGGIOS, ROOT POSITION

	C	G	D	A	E	B	F♯	F	B♭	E♭	A♭	D♭	G♭
♩. = 40													
♩. = 72													
♩. = 104													
♩. =													

MAJOR ARPEGGIOS, 1ST INVERSION

	C	G	D	A	E	B	F♯	F	B♭	E♭	A♭	D♭	G♭
♩. = 40													
♩. = 72													
♩. = 104													
♩. =													

MAJOR ARPEGGIOS, 2ND INVERSION

	C	G	D	A	E	B	F♯	F	B♭	E♭	A♭	D♭	G♭
♩. = 40													
♩. = 72													
♩. = 104													
♩. =													

DOMINANT 7TH ARPEGGIOS

	G	D	A	E	B	F♯	C♯	C	F	B♭	E♭	A♭	D♭
♩ = 52													
♩ = 84													
♩ = 120													
♩ =													

MAJOR CADENCE CHORDS

	C	G	D	A	E	B	F♯	F	B♭	E♭	A♭	D♭	G♭
♩ = 48													
♩ = 66													
♩ = 92													
♩ =													

MINOR

MINOR TRIADS AND INVERSIONS, BLOCK

	a	e	b	f♯	c♯	g♯	d♯	d	g	c	f	b♭	e♭
♩ = 48													
♩ = 66													
♩ = 92													
♩ =													

MINOR TRIADS AND INVERSIONS, BROKEN

	a	e	b	f♯	c♯	g♯	d♯	d	g	c	f	b♭	e♭
♩. = 40													
♩. = 72													
♩. = 104													
♩. =													

MINOR ARPEGGIOS, ROOT POSITION

	a	e	b	f♯	c♯	g♯	d♯	d	g	c	f	b♭	e♭
♩. = 40													
♩. = 72													
♩. = 104													
♩. =													

MINOR ARPEGGIOS, 1ST INVERSION

	a	e	b	f♯	c♯	g♯	d♯	d	g	c	f	b♭	e♭
♩. = 40													
♩. = 72													
♩. = 104													
♩. =													

MINOR ARPEGGIOS, 2ND INVERSION

	a	e	b	f♯	c♯	g♯	d♯	d	g	c	f	b♭	e♭
♩. = 40													
♩. = 72													
♩. = 104													
♩. =													

DIMINISHED 7TH ARPEGGIOS

	g♯	d♯	a♯	e♯	b♯	f𝄪	c𝄪	c♯	f♯	b♮	e♮	a♮	d♮
♩ = 52													
♩ = 84													
♩ = 120													
♩ =													

MINOR CADENCE CHORDS

	a	e	b	f♯	c♯	g♯	d♯	d	g	c	f	b♭	e♭
♩ = 48													
♩ = 66													
♩ = 92													
♩ =													

C Major

* R.H. 4 on B
L.H. 4 on D

QUARTERS in parallel motion, 1 octave

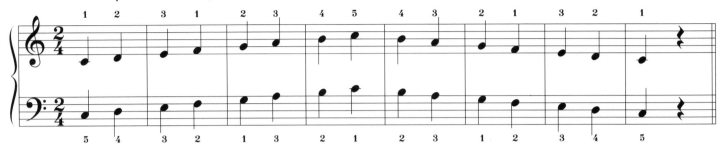

EIGHTHS in parallel motion, 2 octaves

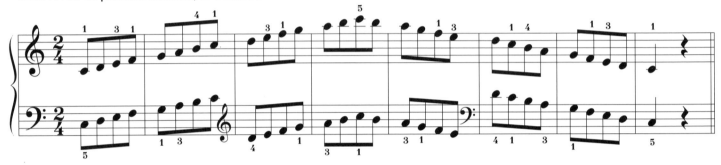

CONTRARY MOTION

THIRDS

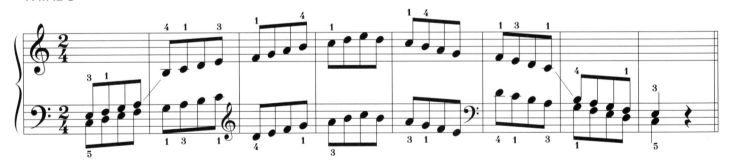

SIXTHS

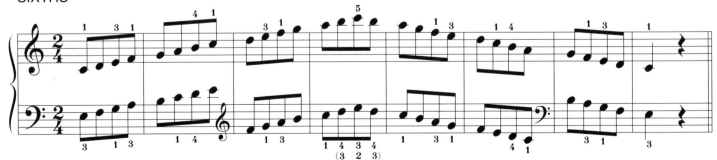

* The fourth finger of each hand generally plays only one note in each octave. Keeping track of the fourth finger aids hands-together scale playing.

TRIADS and INVERSIONS — Block

DOMINANT 7th — Block

TRIADS and INVERSIONS — Broken

ARPEGGIO — Root Position

1st Inversion

2nd Inversion

DOMINANT 7th ARPEGGIO

CADENCE CHORDS

G Major

R.H. 4 on F♯
L.H. 4 on A

QUARTERS in parallel motion, 1 octave

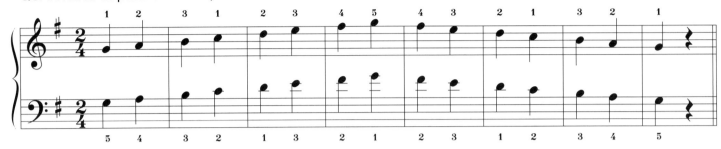

EIGHTHS in parallel motion, 2 octaves

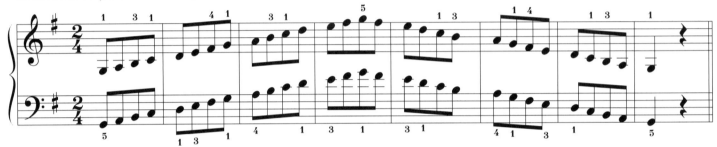

CONTRARY MOTION

THIRDS

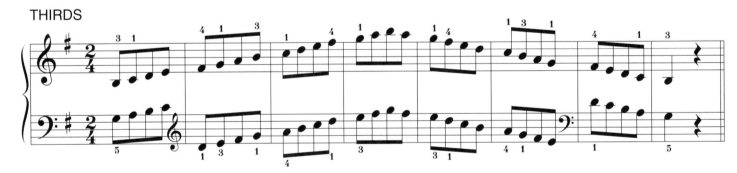

SIXTHS

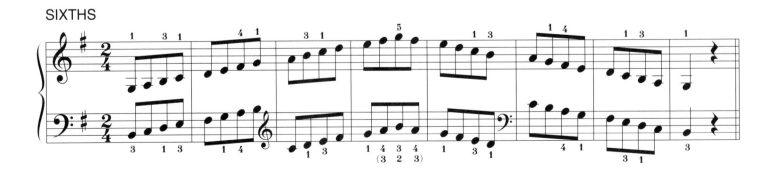

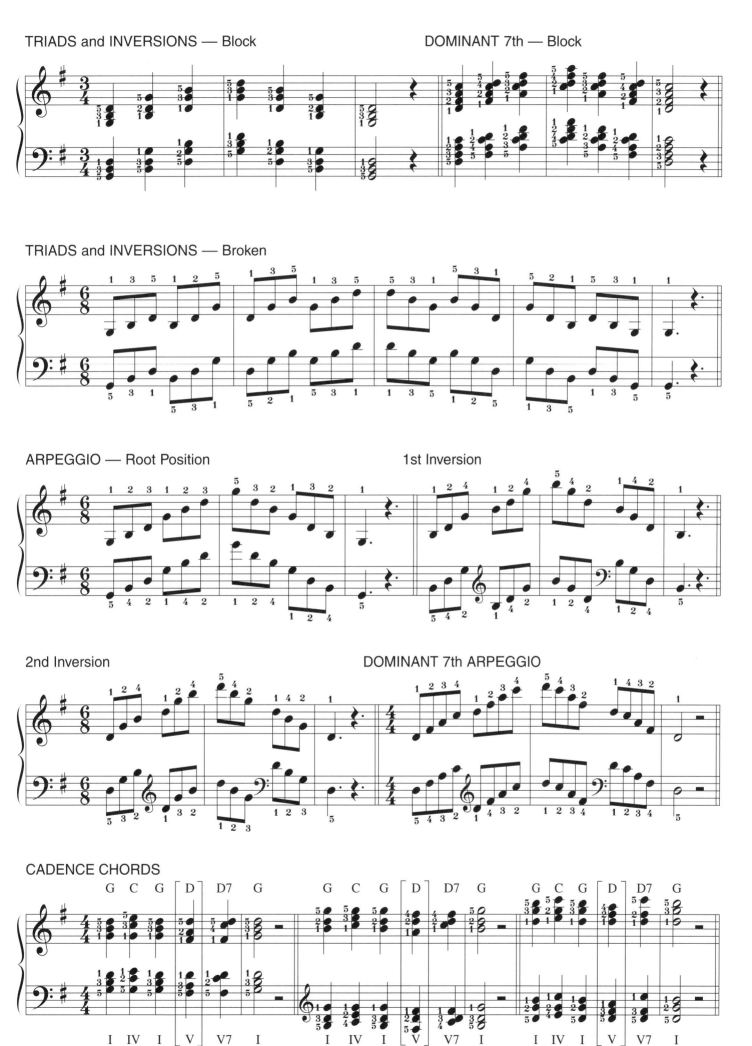

TRIADS and INVERSIONS — Block

DOMINANT 7th — Block

TRIADS and INVERSIONS — Broken

ARPEGGIO — Root Position

1st Inversion

2nd Inversion

DOMINANT 7th ARPEGGIO

CADENCE CHORDS

FJH1132

D Major

R.H. 4 on C#
L.H. 4 on E

QUARTERS in parallel motion, 1 octave

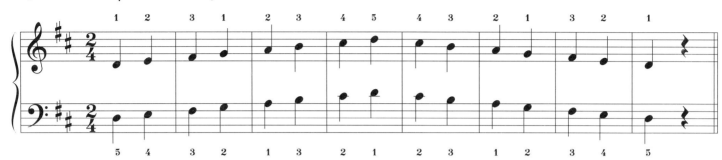

EIGHTHS in parallel motion, 2 octaves

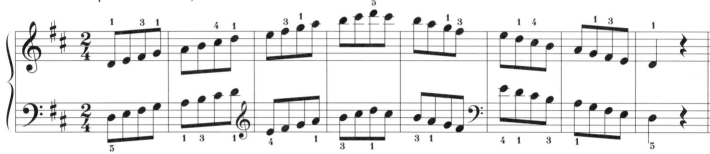

CONTRARY MOTION

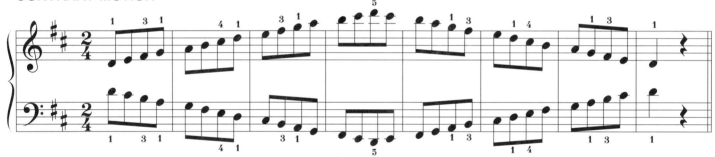

THIRDS

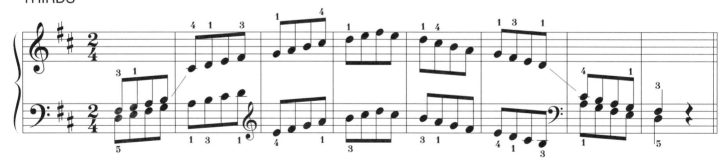

SIXTHS

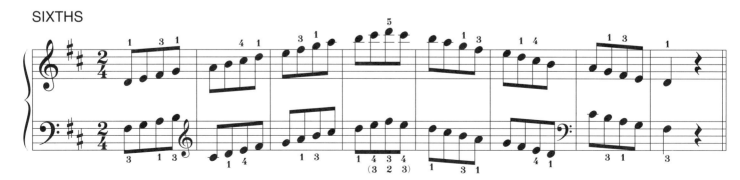

TRIADS and INVERSIONS — Block

DOMINANT 7th — Block

TRIADS and INVERSIONS — Broken

ARPEGGIO — Root Position

1st Inversion

2nd Inversion

DOMINANT 7th ARPEGGIO

CADENCE CHORDS

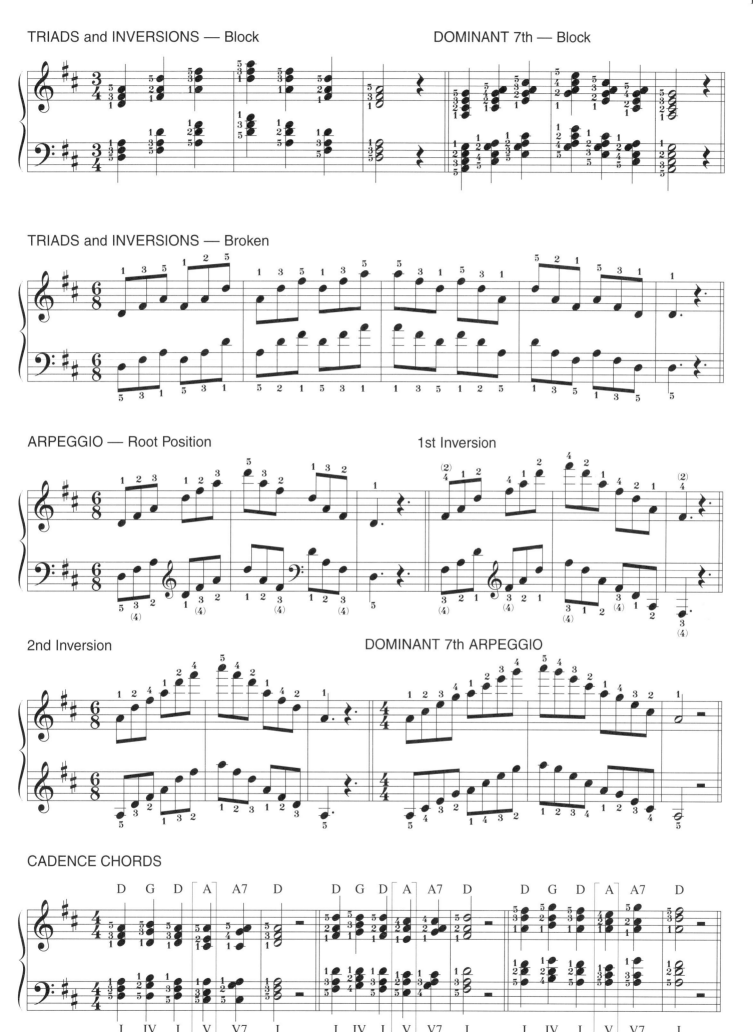

A Major

R.H. 4 on G♯
L.H. 4 on B

QUARTERS in parallel motion, 1 octave

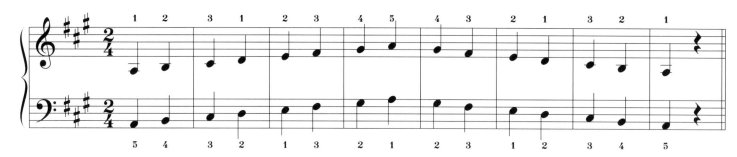

EIGHTHS in parallel motion, 2 octaves

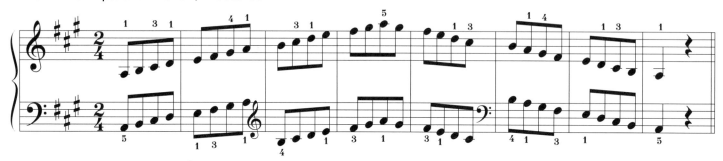

CONTRARY MOTION

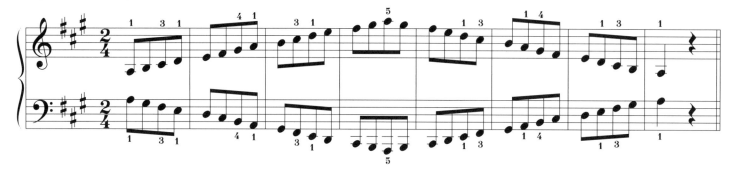

THIRDS

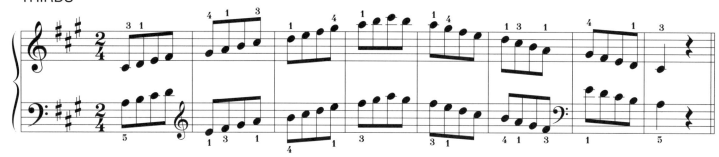

SIXTHS

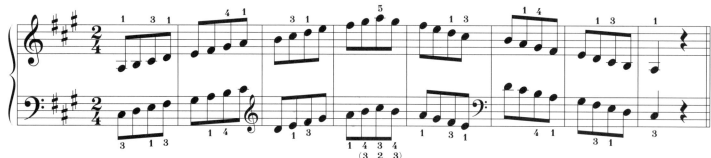

TRIADS and INVERSIONS — Block

DOMINANT 7th — Block

TRIADS and INVERSIONS — Broken

ARPEGGIO — Root Position

1st Inversion

2nd Inversion

DOMINANT 7th ARPEGGIO

CADENCE CHORDS

E Major

R.H. 4 on D♯
L.H. 4 on F♯

QUARTERS in parallel motion, 1 octave

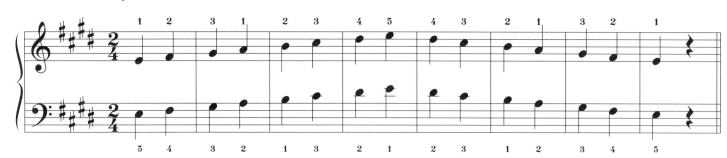

EIGHTHS in parallel motion, 2 octaves

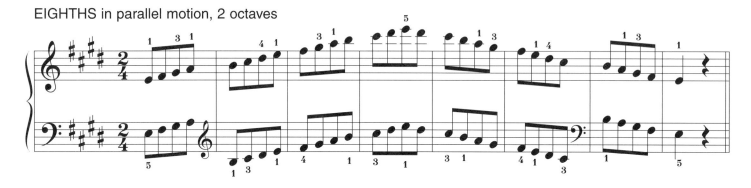

CONTRARY MOTION

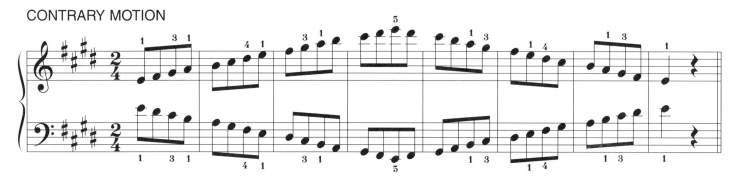

THIRDS

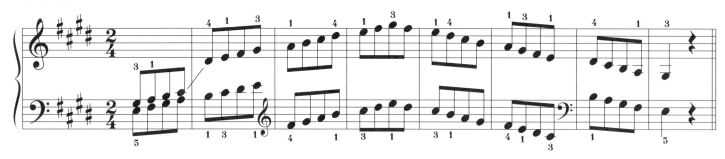

SIXTHS

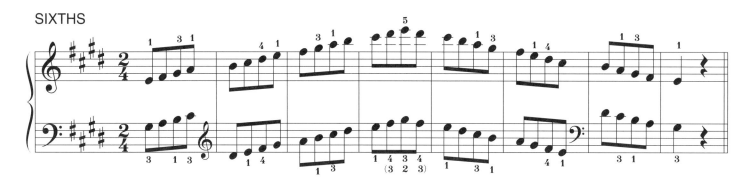

TRIADS and INVERSIONS — Block   DOMINANT 7th — Block

TRIADS and INVERSIONS — Broken

ARPEGGIO — Root Position   1st Inversion

2nd Inversion   DOMINANT 7th ARPEGGIO

CADENCE CHORDS

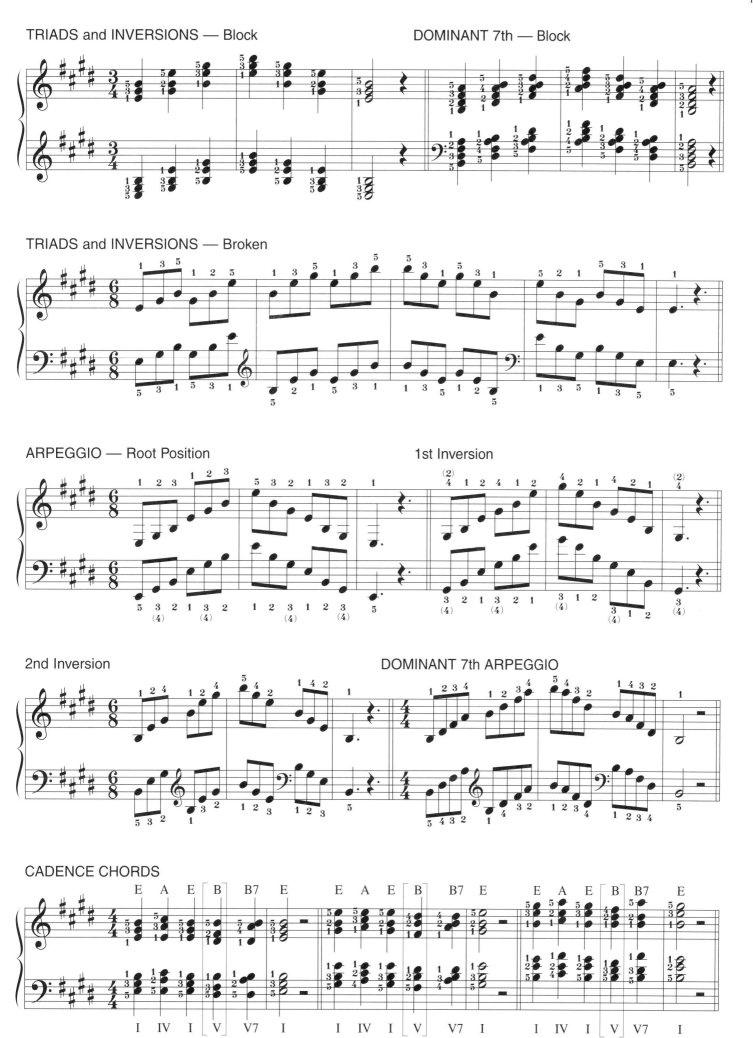

B Major
(ENHARMONIC OF Cb MAJOR)

R.H. 4 on A♯

L.H. 4 on both B and F♯

QUARTERS in parallel motion, 1 octave

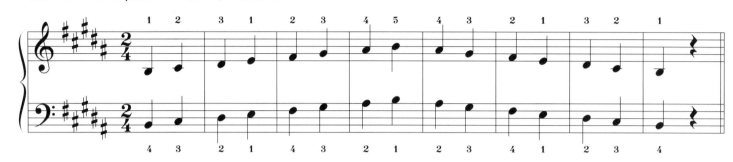

EIGHTHS in parallel motion, 2 octaves

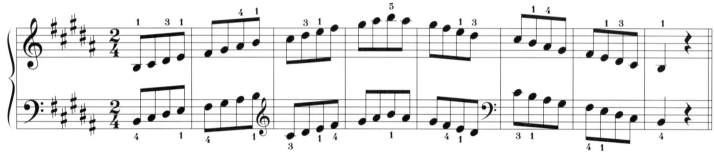

CONTRARY MOTION

THIRDS

SIXTHS

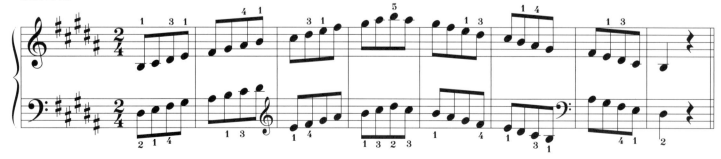

FJH1132

TRIADS and INVERSIONS — Block

DOMINANT 7th — Block

TRIADS and INVERSIONS — Broken

ARPEGGIO — Root Position

1st Inversion

2nd Inversion

DOMINANT 7th ARPEGGIO

CADENCE CHORDS

F♯ Major

R.H. 4 on A♯
L.H. 4 on F♯

QUARTERS in parallel motion, 1 octave

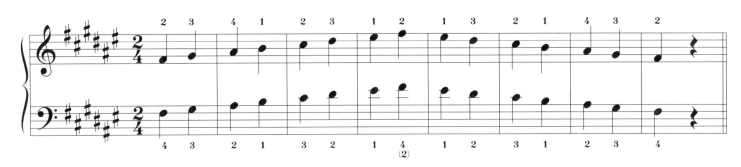

EIGHTHS in parallel motion, 2 octaves

CONTRARY MOTION

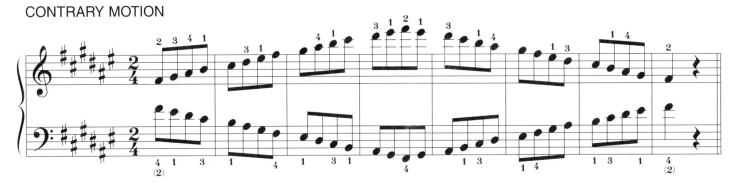

THIRDS

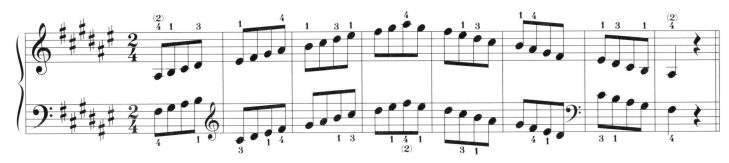

SIXTHS

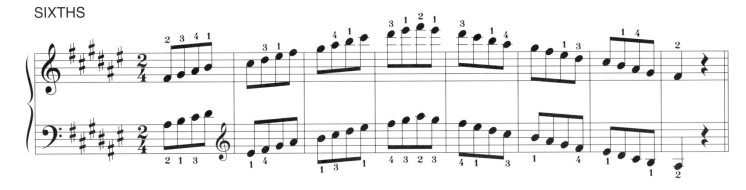

TRIADS and INVERSIONS — Block   DOMINANT 7th — Block

TRIADS and INVERSIONS — Broken

ARPEGGIO — Root Position   1st Inversion

2nd Inversion   DOMINANT 7th ARPEGGIO

CADENCE CHORDS

FJH1132

F Major

*R.H. 4 on B♭
L.H. 4 on G

QUARTERS in parallel motion, 1 octave

EIGHTHS in parallel motion, 2 octaves

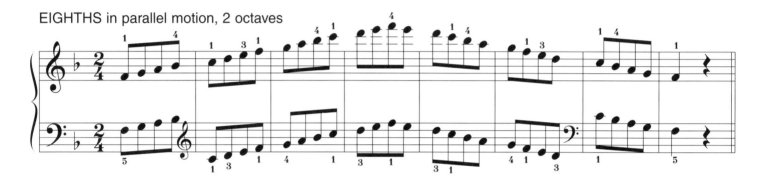

CONTRARY MOTION

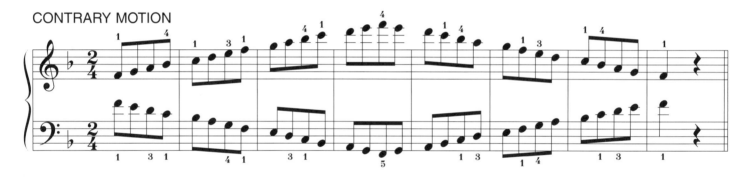

THIRDS

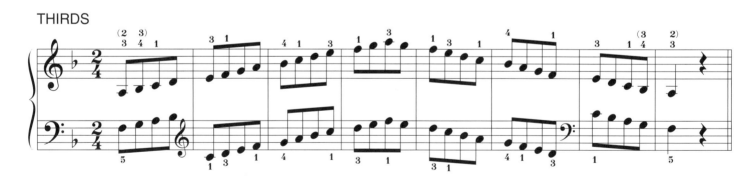

SIXTHS

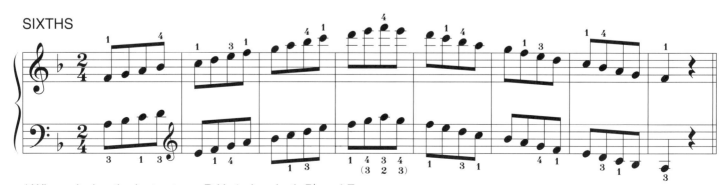

* When playing the last octave, R.H. 4 plays both B♭ and F.

TRIADS and INVERSIONS — Block   DOMINANT 7th — Block

TRIADS and INVERSIONS — Broken

ARPEGGIO — Root Position   1st Inversion

2nd Inversion   DOMINANT 7th ARPEGGIO

CADENCE CHORDS

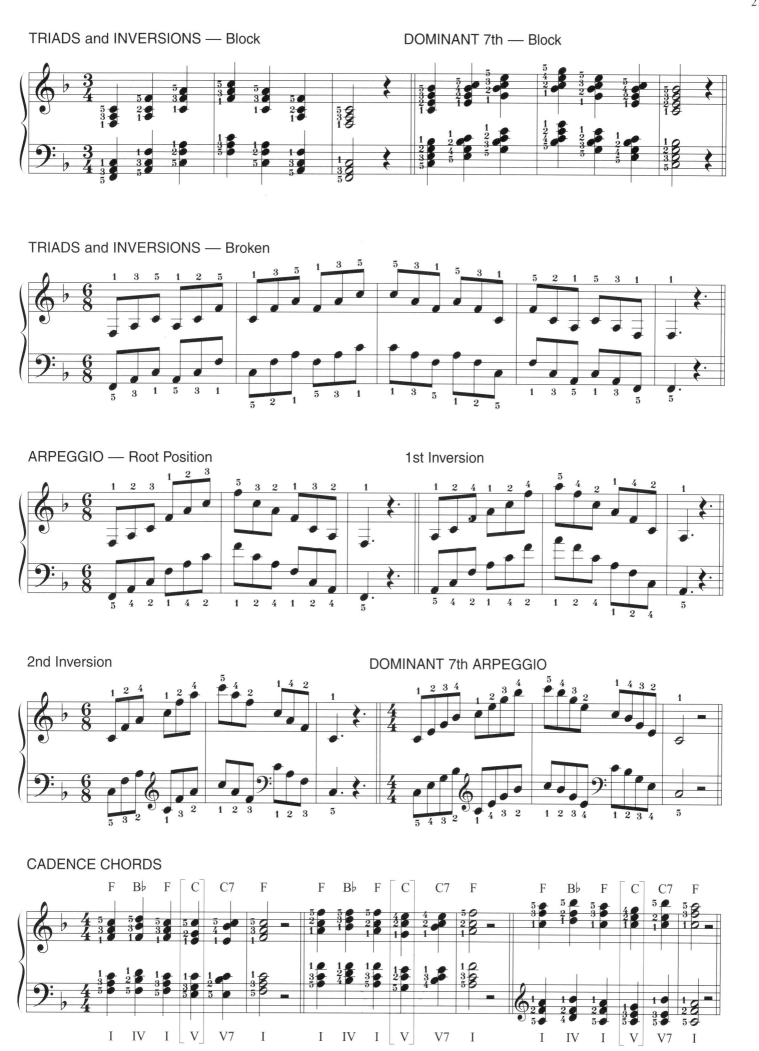

B♭ Major

R.H. 4 on B♭
L.H. 4 on E♭

QUARTERS in parallel motion, 1 octave

EIGHTHS in parallel motion, 2 octaves

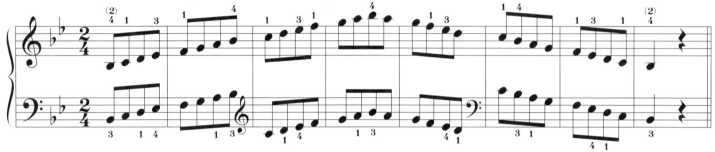

CONTRARY MOTION

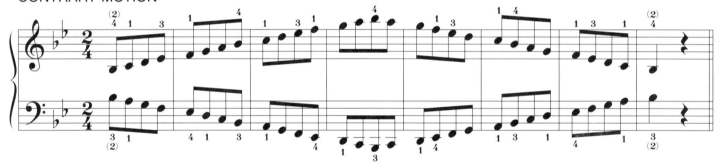

THIRDS

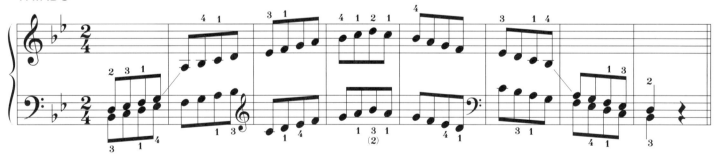

SIXTHS

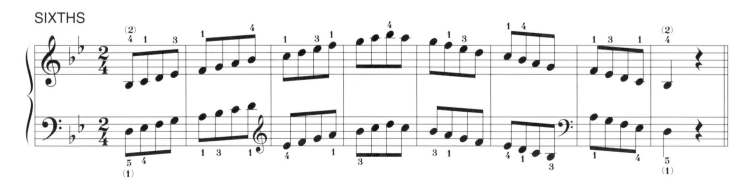

TRIADS and INVERSIONS — Block

DOMINANT 7th — Block

TRIADS and INVERSIONS — Broken

ARPEGGIO — Root Position

1st Inversion

2nd Inversion

DOMINANT 7th ARPEGGIO

CADENCE CHORDS

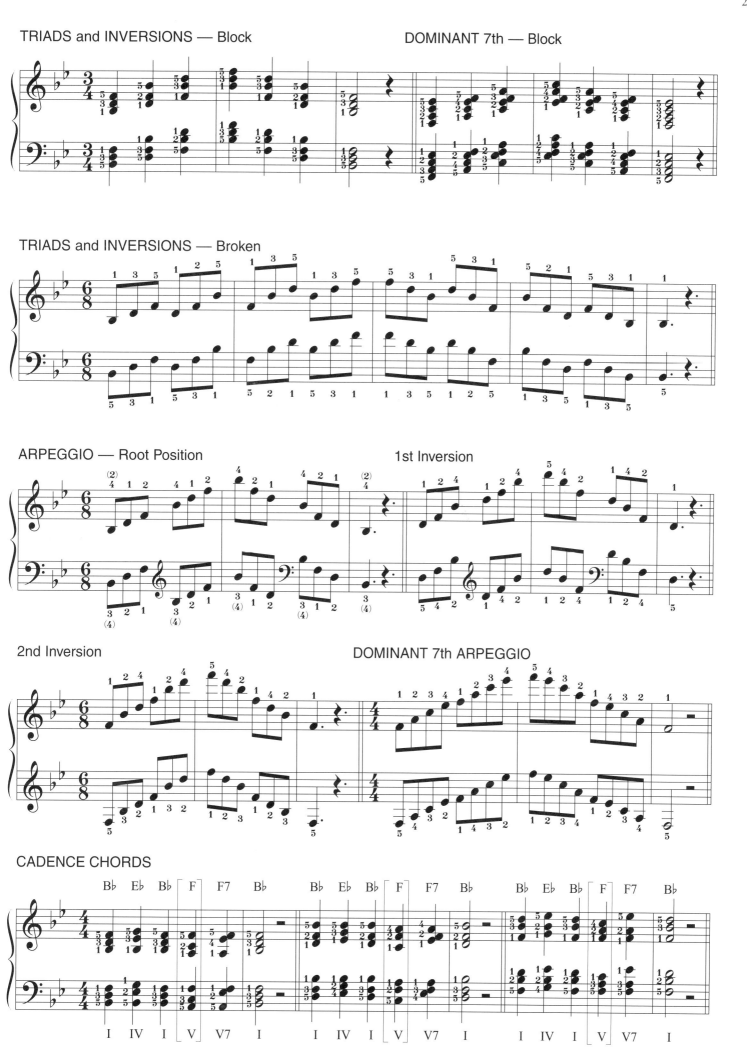

FJH1132

E♭ Major

R.H. 4 on B♭
L.H. 4 on A♭

QUARTERS in parallel motion, 1 octave

EIGHTHS in parallel motion, 2 octaves

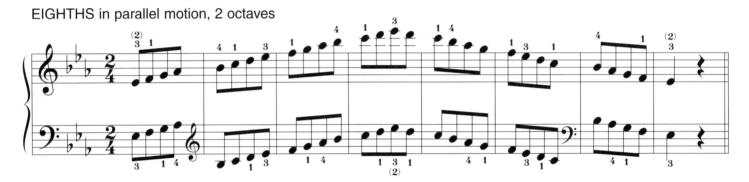

CONTRARY MOTION

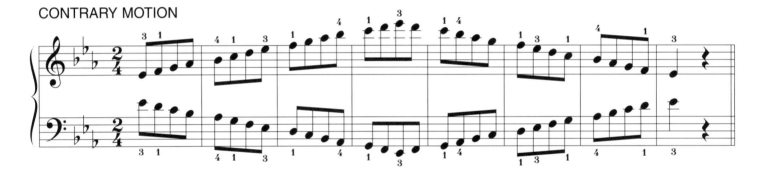

THIRDS

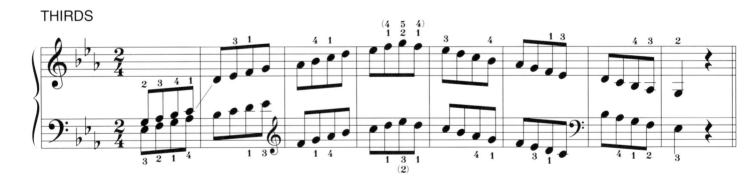

SIXTHS

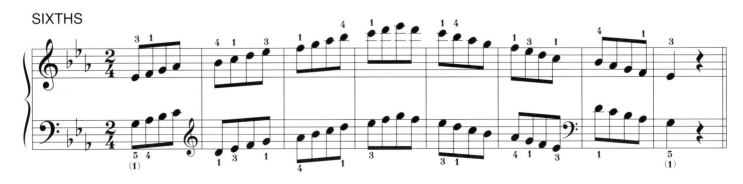

TRIADS and INVERSIONS — Block

DOMINANT 7th — Block

TRIADS and INVERSIONS — Broken

ARPEGGIO — Root Position

1st Inversion

2nd Inversion

DOMINANT 7th ARPEGGIO

CADENCE CHORDS

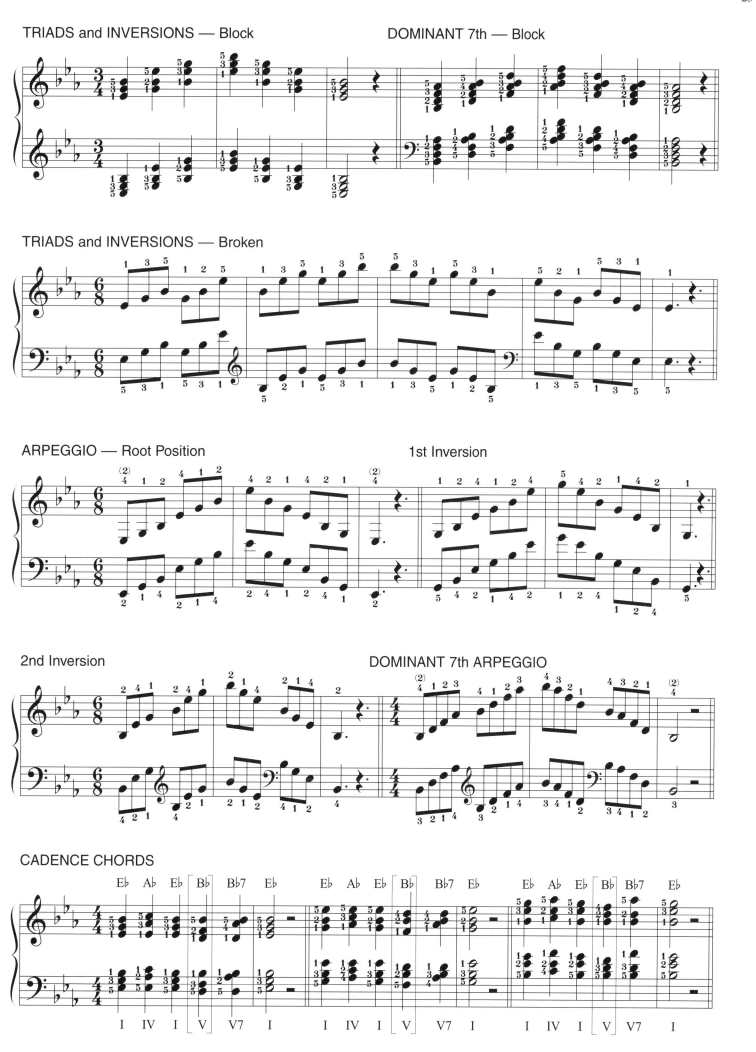

A♭ Major

R.H. 4 on B♭
L.H. 4 on D♭

QUARTERS in parallel motion, 1 octave

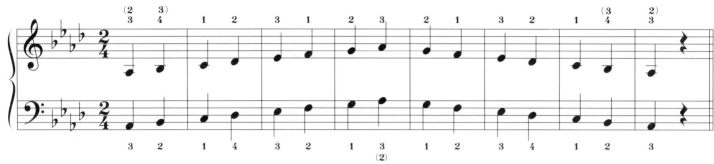

EIGHTHS in parallel motion, 2 octaves

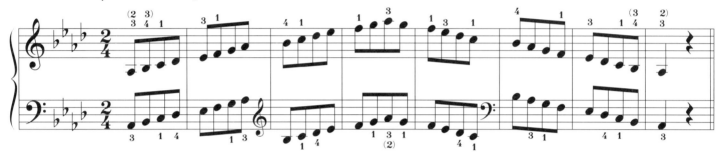

CONTRARY MOTION

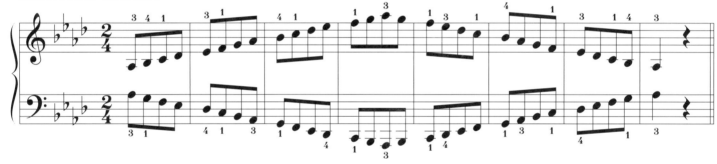

THIRDS

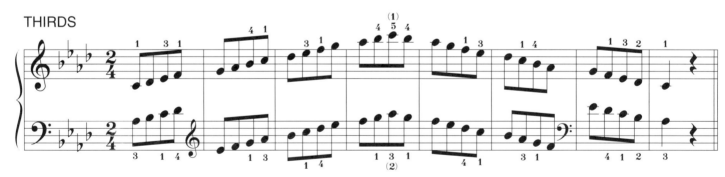

SIXTHS

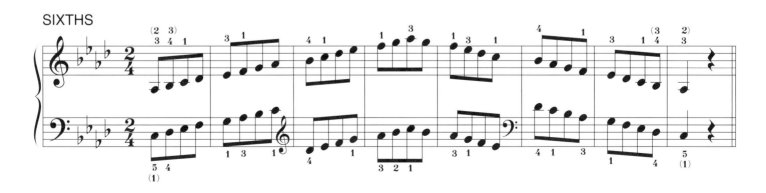

FJH1132

TRIADS and INVERSIONS — Block

DOMINANT 7th — Block

TRIADS and INVERSIONS — Broken

ARPEGGIO — Root Position

1st Inversion

2nd Inversion

DOMINANT 7th ARPEGGIO

CADENCE CHORDS

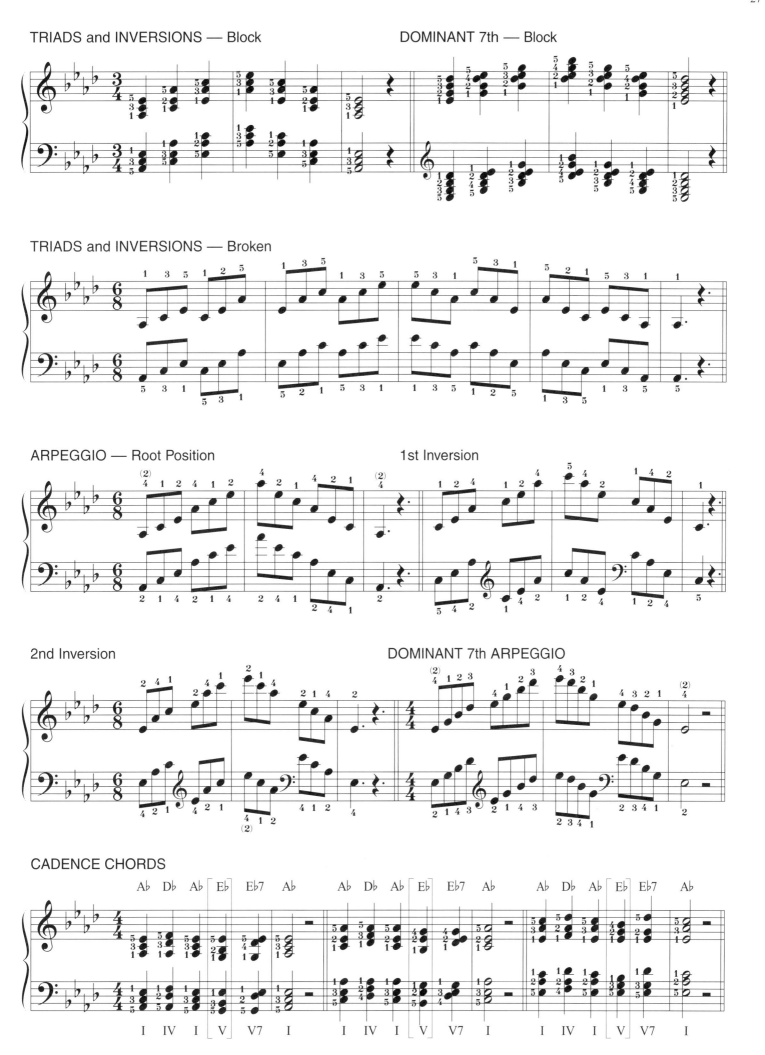

D♭ Major
(ENHARMONIC OF C♯ MAJOR)

R.H. 4 on B♭

L.H. 4 on G♭

QUARTERS in parallel motion, 1 octave

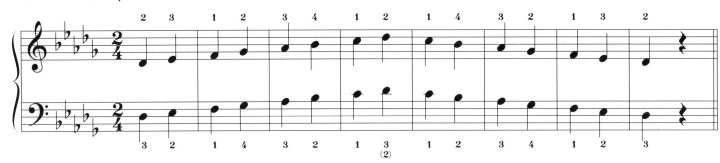

EIGHTHS in parallel motion, 2 octaves

CONTRARY MOTION

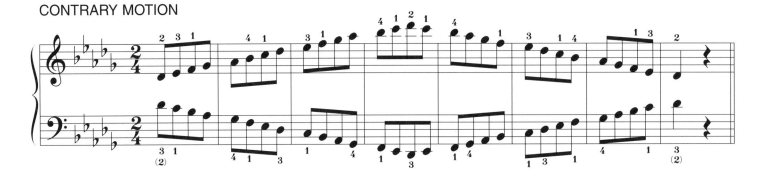

THIRDS

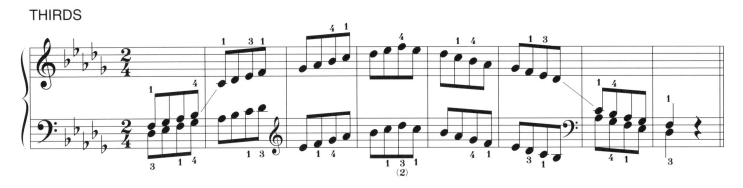

SIXTHS

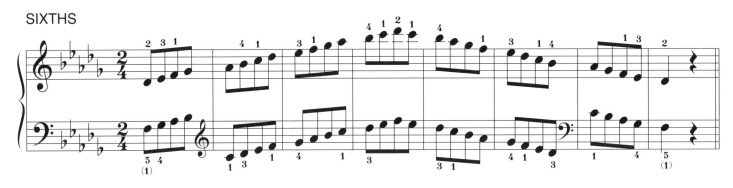

TRIADS and INVERSIONS — Block

DOMINANT 7th — Block

TRIADS and INVERSIONS — Broken

ARPEGGIO — Root Position

1st Inversion

2nd Inversion

DOMINANT 7th ARPEGGIO

CADENCE CHORDS

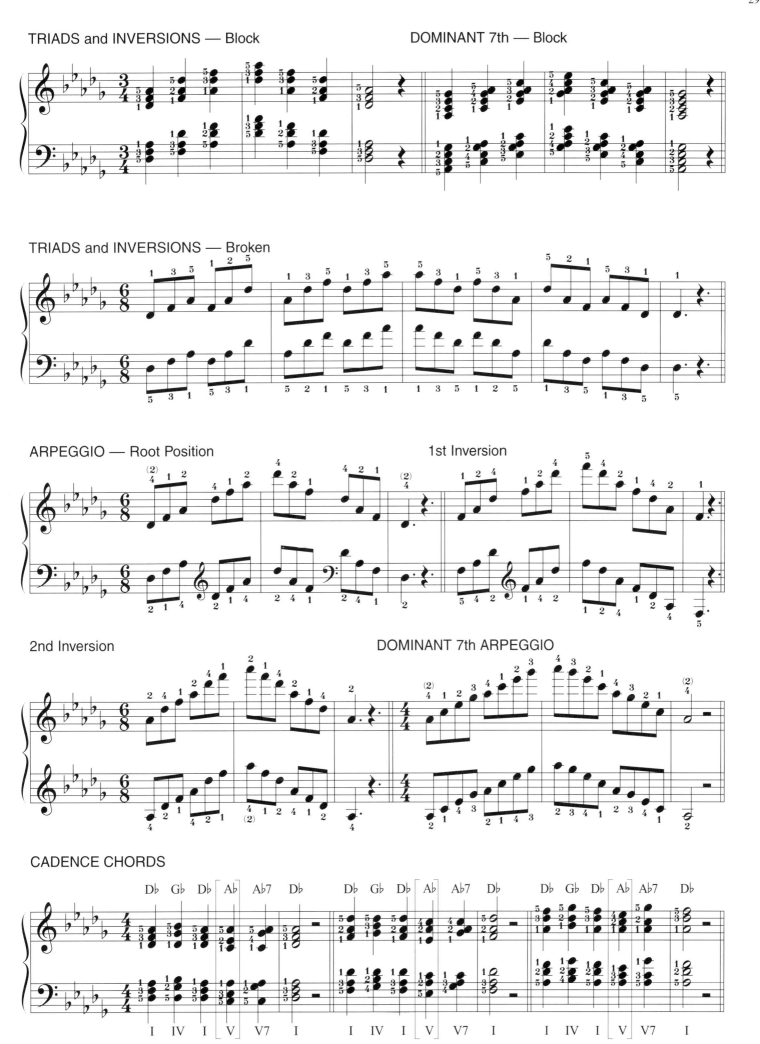

G♭ Major

R.H. 4 on B♭
L.H. 4 on G♭

QUARTERS in parallel motion, 1 octave

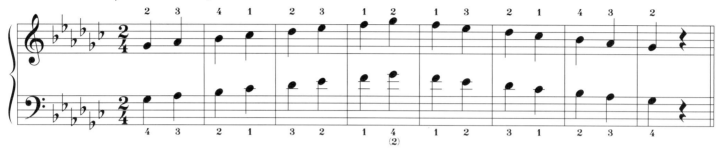

EIGHTHS in parallel motion, 2 octaves

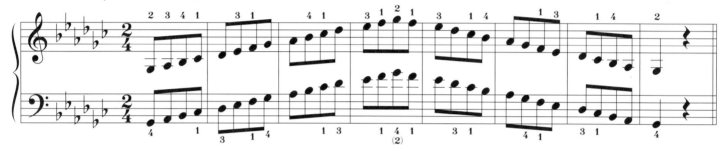

CONTRARY MOTION

THIRDS

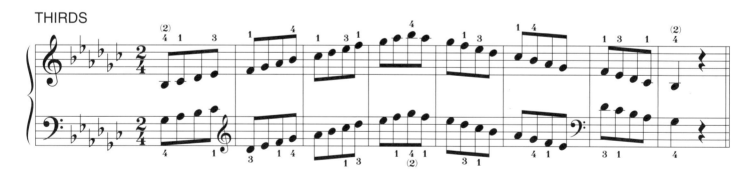

SIXTHS

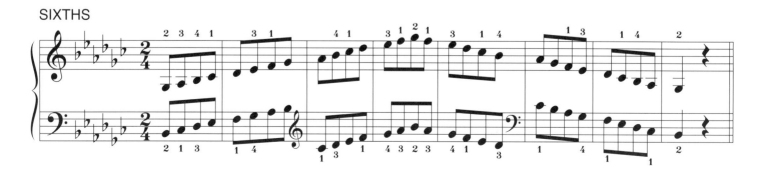

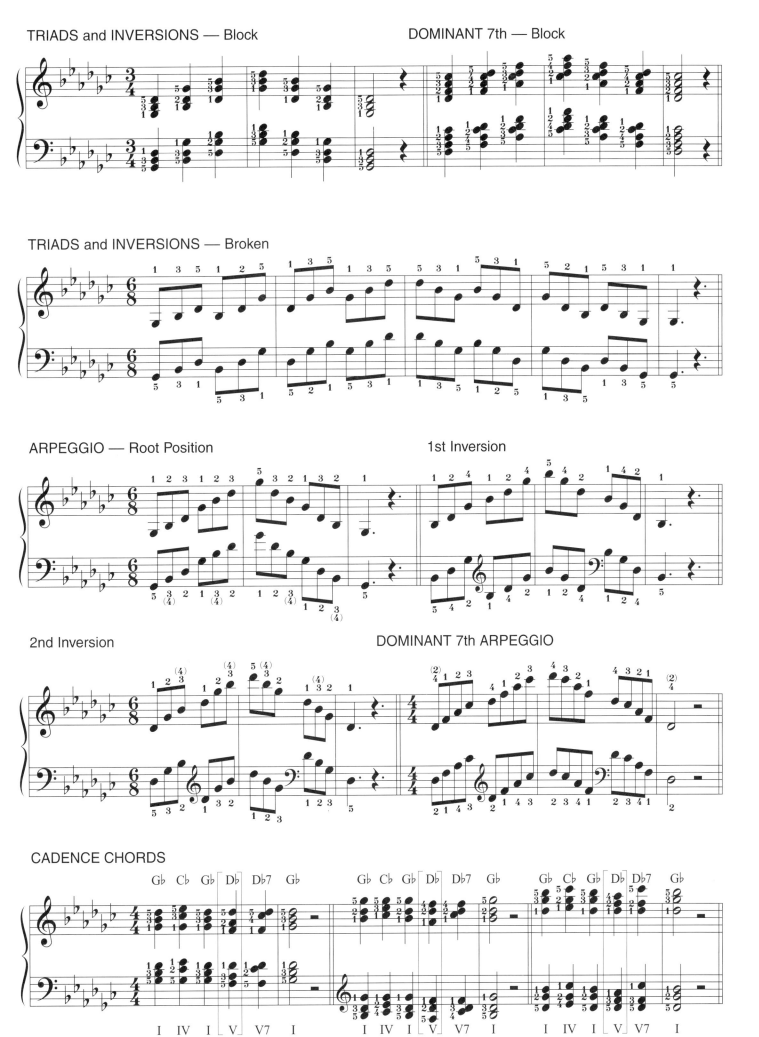

A Minor
(RELATIVE OF C MAJOR)

R.H. 4 on G or G#
L.H. 4 on B

NATURAL MINOR — Quarters, 1 octave

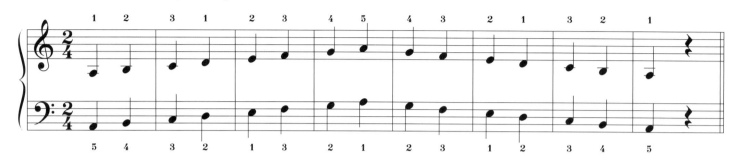

NATURAL MINOR — Eighths, 2 octaves

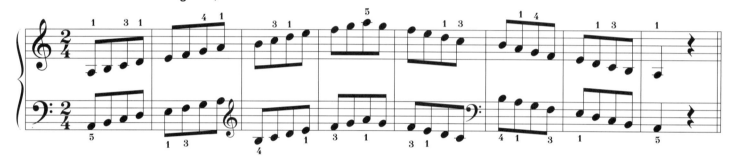

HARMONIC MINOR — Parallel motion

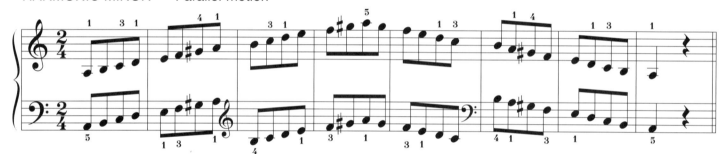

HARMONIC MINOR — Contrary motion

MELODIC MINOR

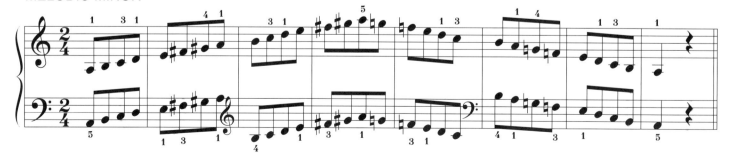

E Minor
(Relative of G Major)

R.H. 4 on D or D♯

L.H. 4 on F♯

NATURAL MINOR — Quarters, 1 octave

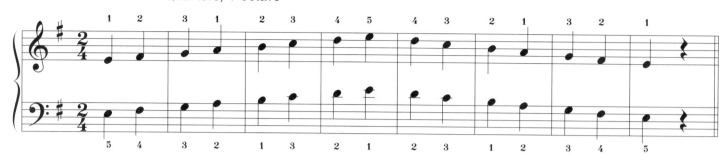

NATURAL MINOR — Eighths, 2 octaves

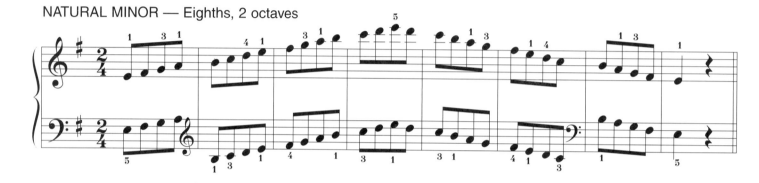

HARMONIC MINOR — Parallel motion

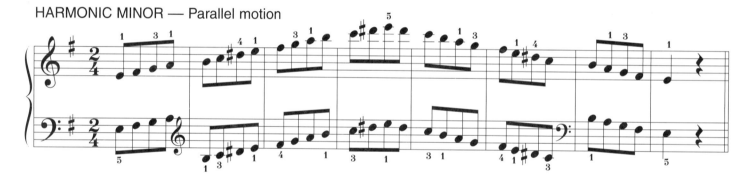

HARMONIC MINOR — Contrary motion

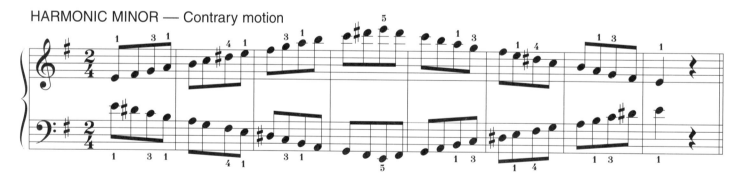

MELODIC MINOR

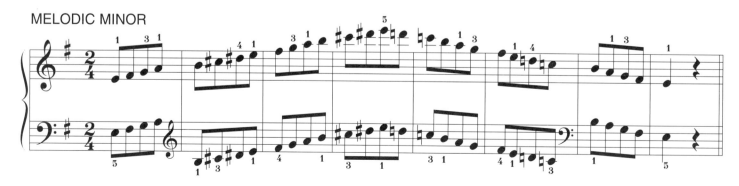

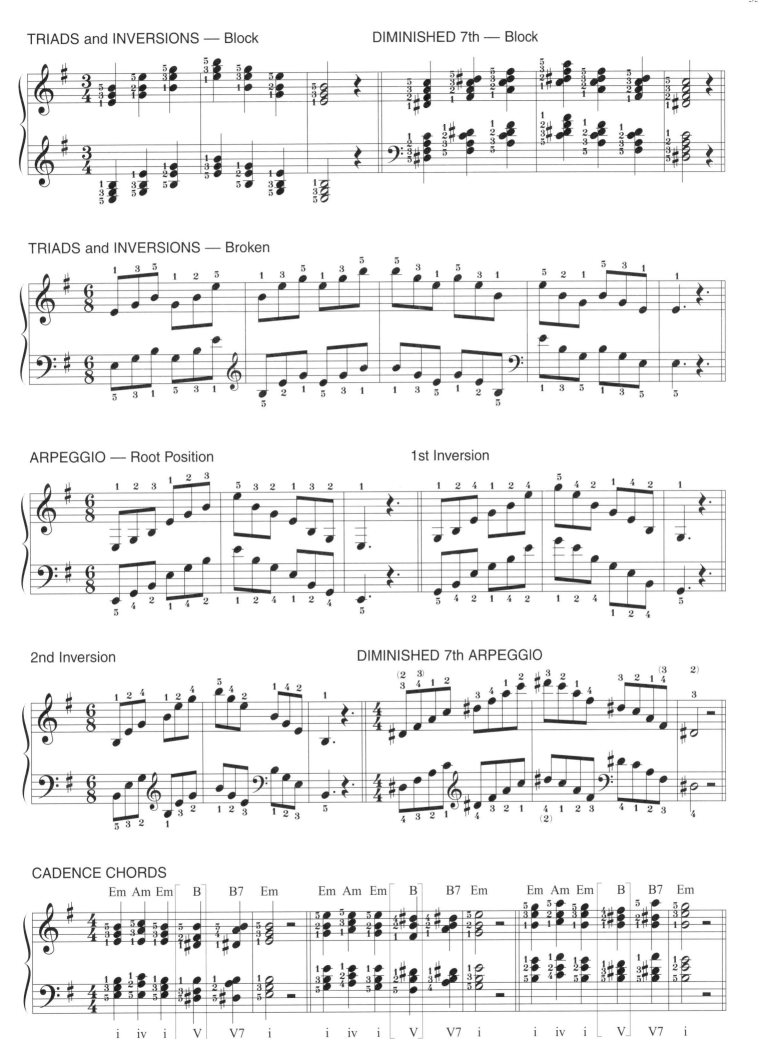

TRIADS and INVERSIONS — Block

DIMINISHED 7th — Block

TRIADS and INVERSIONS — Broken

ARPEGGIO — Root Position

1st Inversion

2nd Inversion

DIMINISHED 7th ARPEGGIO

CADENCE CHORDS

B Minor
(RELATIVE OF D MAJOR)

R.H. 4 on A or A#

L.H. 4 on B and F#

NATURAL MINOR — Quarters, 1 octave

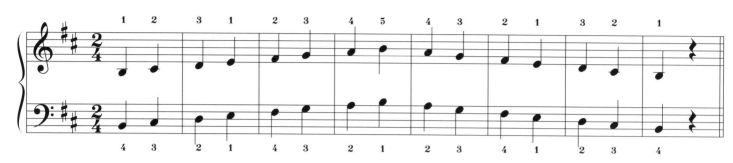

NATURAL MINOR — Eighths, 2 octaves

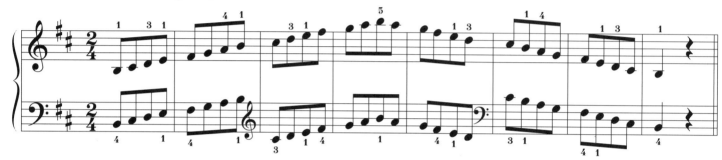

HARMONIC MINOR — Parallel motion

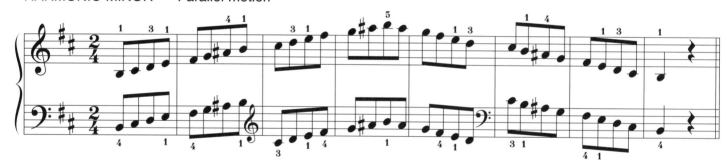

HARMONIC MINOR — Contrary motion

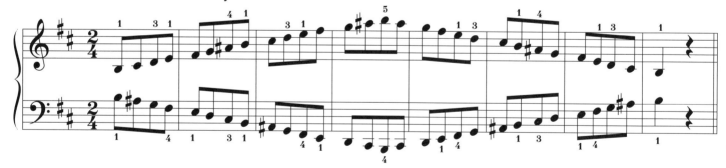

MELODIC MINOR

TRIADS and INVERSIONS — Block

DIMINISHED 7th — Block

TRIADS and INVERSIONS — Broken

ARPEGGIO — Root Position

1st Inversion

2nd Inversion

DIMINISHED 7th ARPEGGIO

CADENCE CHORDS

F♯ Minor
(RELATIVE OF A MAJOR)

*R.H. 4 on G♯ or D♯

L.H. 4 on F♯

NATURAL MINOR — Quarters, 1 octave

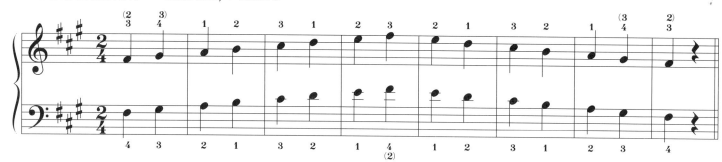

NATURAL MINOR — Eighths, 2 octaves

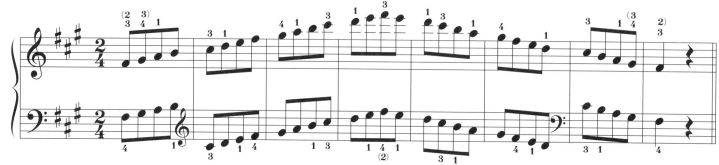

HARMONIC MINOR — Parallel motion

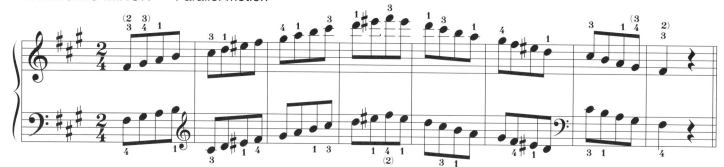

HARMONIC MINOR — Contrary motion

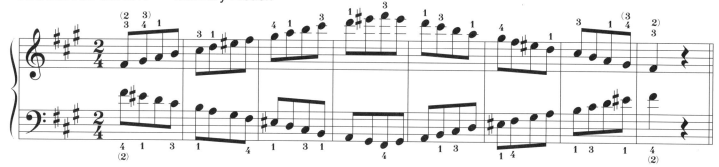

MELODIC MINOR

* R.H. fingering in ascending melodic minor: 3 4 1 2 3 4 1 2 .

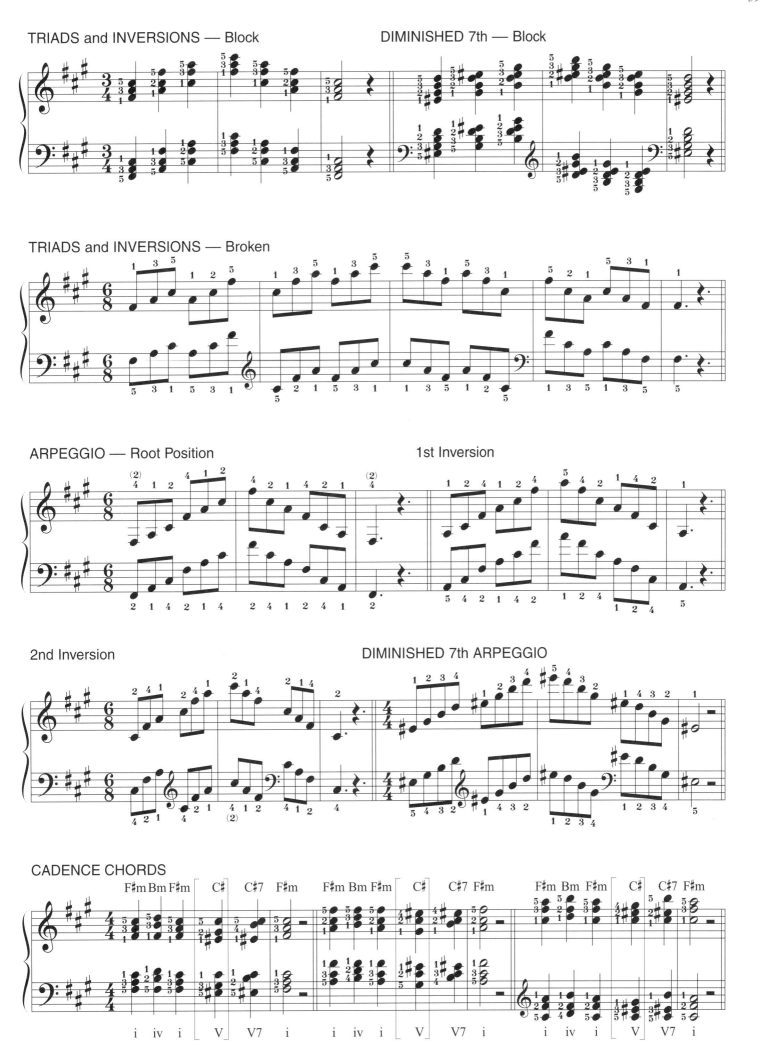

FJH1132

C♯ Minor
(RELATIVE OF E MAJOR)

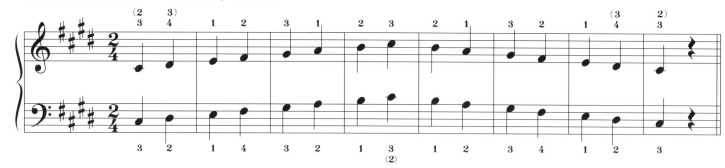

> *R.H. 4 on D♯ or A♯
> L.H. 4 on F♯

NATURAL MINOR — Quarters, 1 octave

NATURAL MINOR — Eighths, 2 octaves

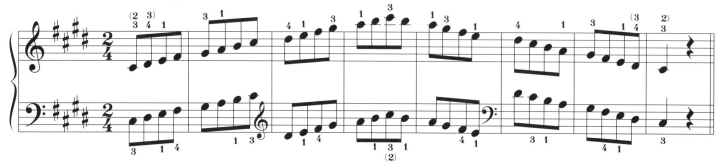

HARMONIC MINOR — Parallel motion

HARMONIC MINOR — Contrary motion

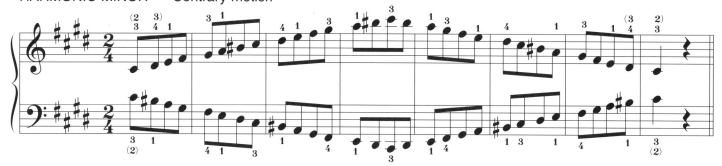

MELODIC MINOR

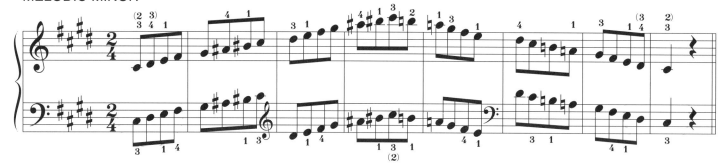

* R.H. fingering in ascending melodic minor: 3 4 1 2 3 4 1 2 .

TRIADS and INVERSIONS — Block

DIMINISHED 7th — Block

TRIADS and INVERSIONS — Broken

ARPEGGIO — Root Position

1st Inversion

2nd Inversion

DIMINISHED 7th ARPEGGIO

CADENCE CHORDS

G# Minor
(Relative of B Major)

R.H. 4 on A#
*L.H. 4 on C# or F#

NATURAL MINOR — Quarters, 1 octave

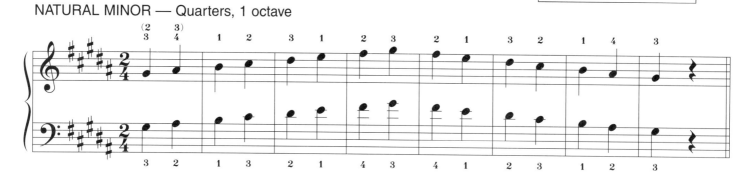

NATURAL MINOR — Eighths, 2 octaves

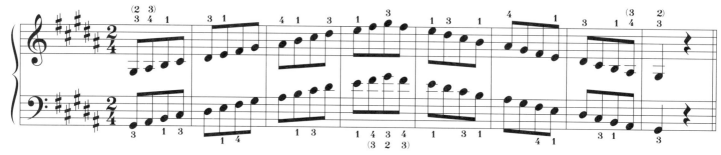

HARMONIC MINOR — Parallel motion

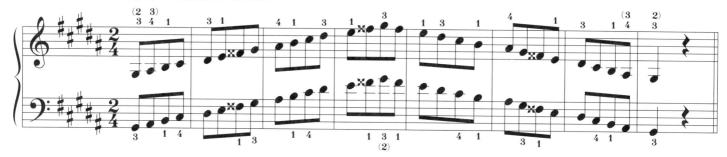

HARMONIC MINOR — Contrary motion

MELODIC MINOR

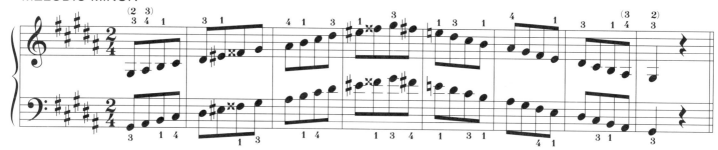

* L.H. fingering in descending melodic minor: 3 4 1 2 3 1 2 3 .

TRIADS and INVERSIONS — Block

DIMINISHED 7th — Block

TRIADS and INVERSIONS — Broken

ARPEGGIO — Root Position

1st Inversion

2nd Inversion

DIMINISHED 7th ARPEGGIO

CADENCE CHORDS

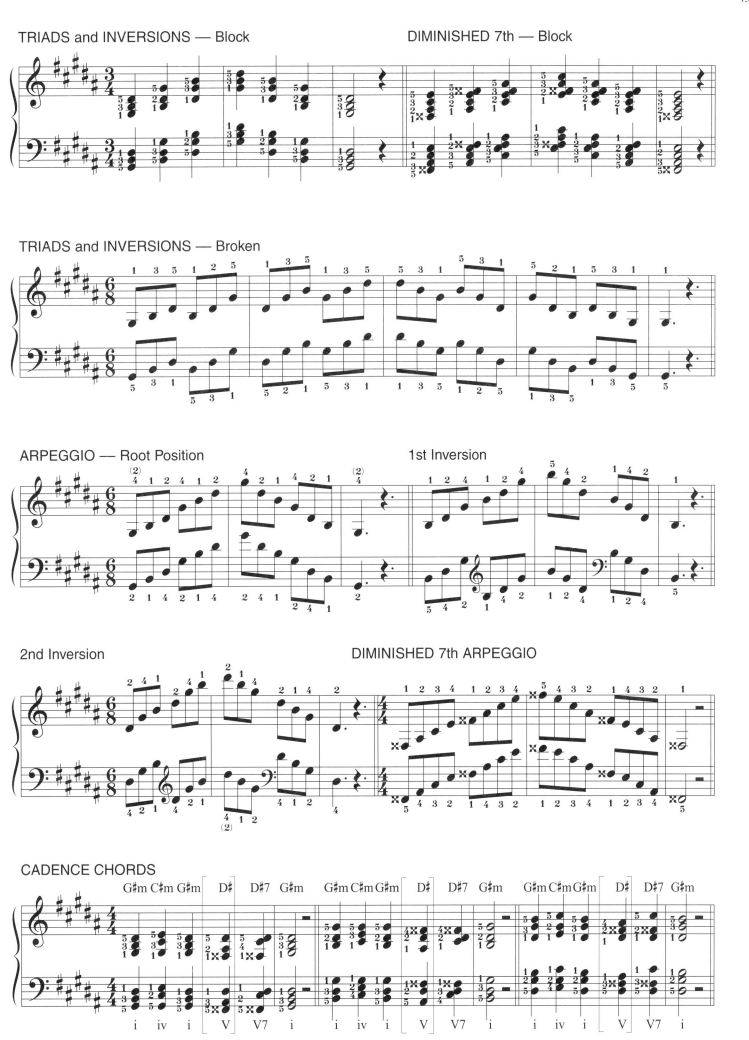

D♯ Minor
RELATIVE OF F♯ MAJOR (G♭ MAJOR)

R.H. 4 on A♯

L.H. 4 on F♯

NATURAL MINOR — Quarters, 1 octave

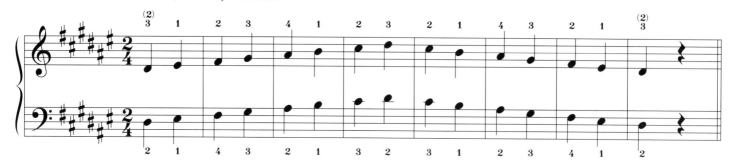

NATURAL MINOR — Eighths, 2 octaves

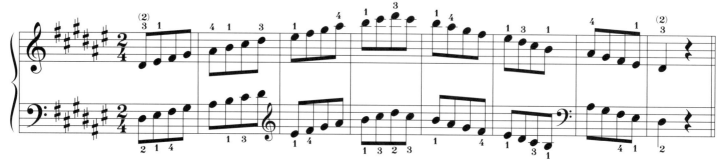

HARMONIC MINOR — Parallel motion

HARMONIC MINOR — Contrary motion

MELODIC MINOR

D Minor
(RELATIVE OF F MAJOR)

R.H. 4 on C or C#

L.H. 4 on E

NATURAL MINOR — Quarters, 1 octave

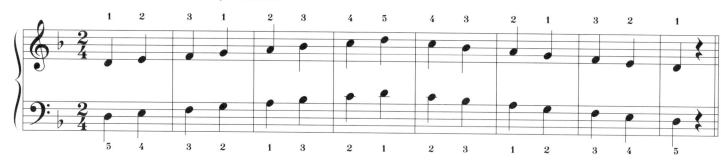

NATURAL MINOR — Eighths, 2 octaves

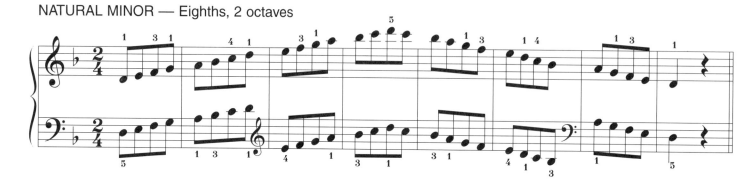

HARMONIC MINOR — Parallel motion

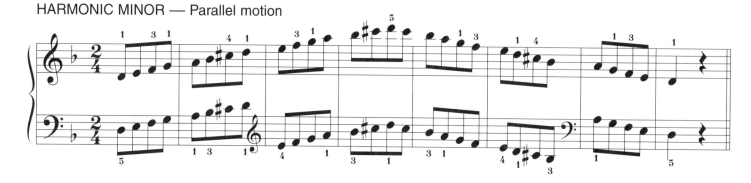

HARMONIC MINOR — Contrary motion

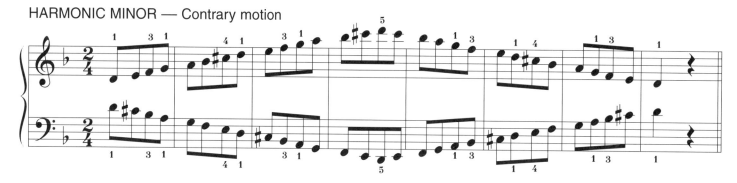

MELODIC MINOR

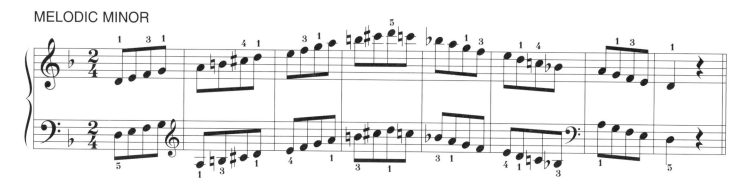

TRIADS and INVERSIONS — Block

DIMINISHED 7th — Block

TRIADS and INVERSIONS — Broken

ARPEGGIO — Root Position

1st Inversion

2nd Inversion

DIMINISHED 7th ARPEGGIO

CADENCE CHORDS

G Minor
(RELATIVE OF B♭ MAJOR)

R.H. 4 on F or F♯
L.H. 4 on A

NATURAL MINOR — Quarters, 1 octave

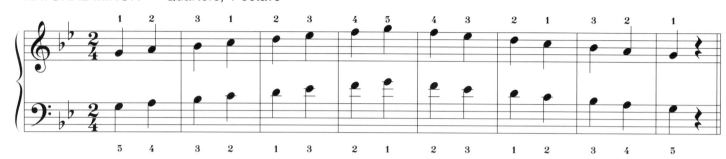

NATURAL MINOR — Eighths, 2 octaves

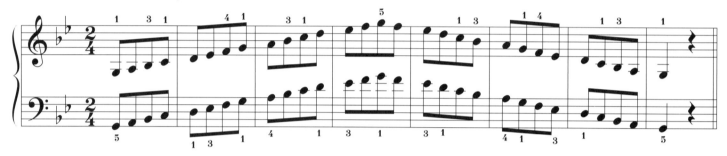

HARMONIC MINOR — Parallel motion

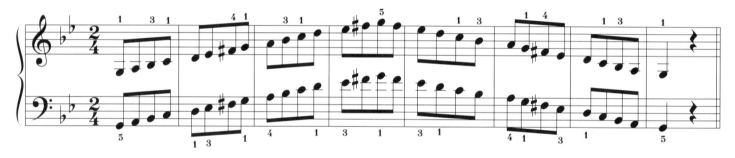

HARMONIC MINOR — Contrary motion

MELODIC MINOR

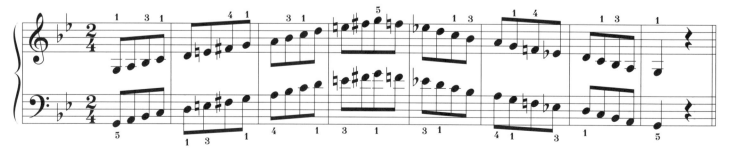

TRIADS and INVERSIONS — Block
DIMINISHED 7th — Block

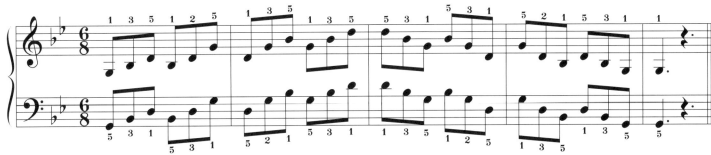

TRIADS and INVERSIONS — Broken

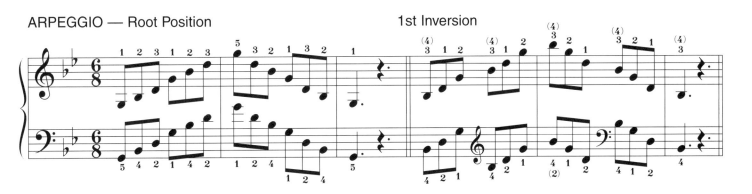

ARPEGGIO — Root Position
1st Inversion

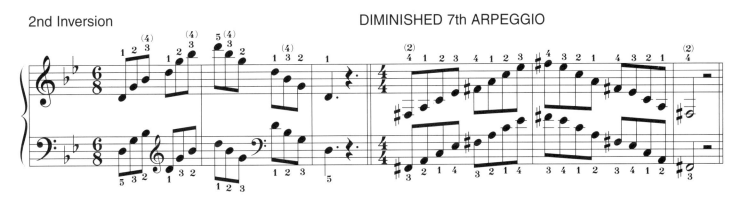

2nd Inversion
DIMINISHED 7th ARPEGGIO

CADENCE CHORDS

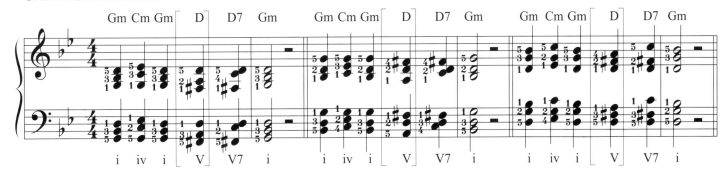

C Minor
(RELATIVE OF Eb MAJOR)

R.H. 4 on B or Bb

L.H. 4 on D

NATURAL MINOR — Quarters, 1 octave

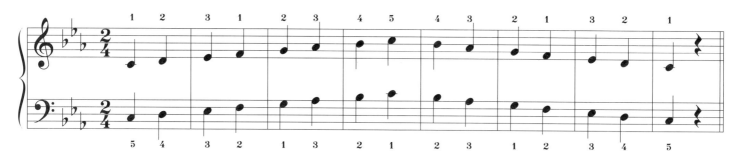

NATURAL MINOR — Eighths, 2 octaves

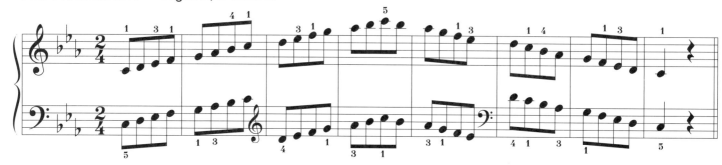

HARMONIC MINOR — Parallel motion

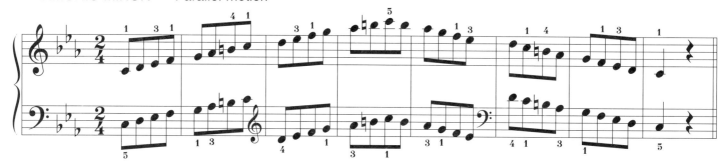

HARMONIC MINOR — Contrary motion

MELODIC MINOR

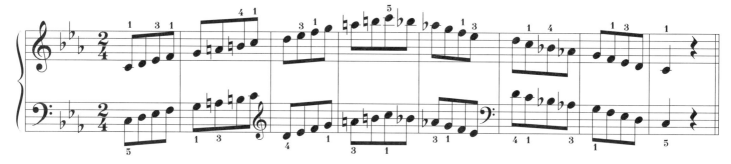

TRIADS and INVERSIONS — Block

DIMINISHED 7th — Block

TRIADS and INVERSIONS — Broken

ARPEGGIO — Root Position

1st Inversion

2nd Inversion

DIMINISHED 7th ARPEGGIO

CADENCE CHORDS

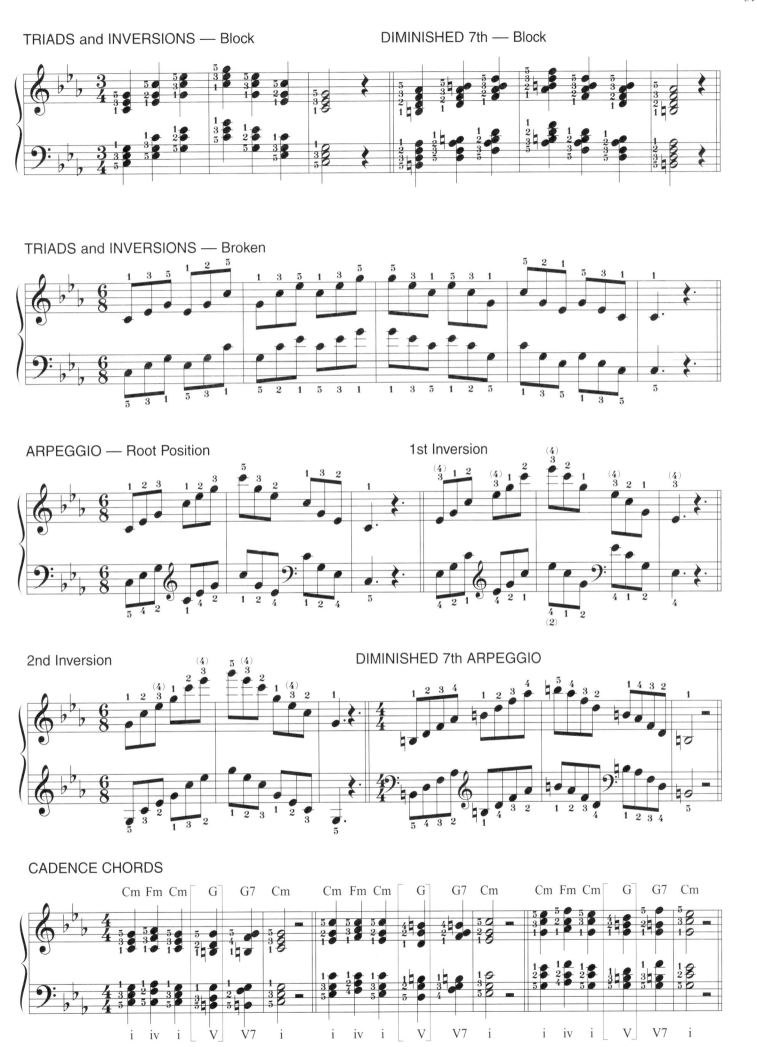

F Minor
(RELATIVE OF A♭ MAJOR)

R.H. 4 on B♭

L.H. 4 on G

NATURAL MINOR — Quarters, 1 octave

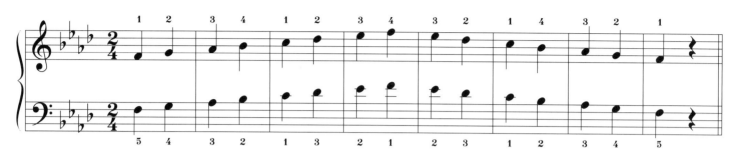

NATURAL MINOR — Eighths, 2 octaves

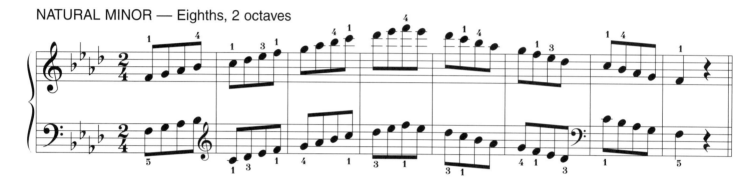

HARMONIC MINOR — Parallel motion

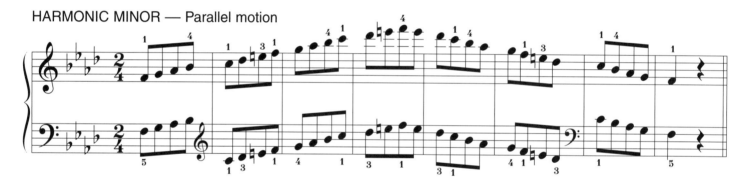

HARMONIC MINOR — Contrary motion

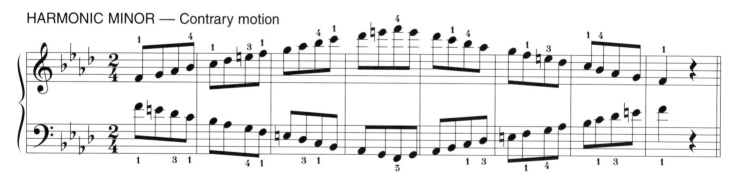

MELODIC MINOR

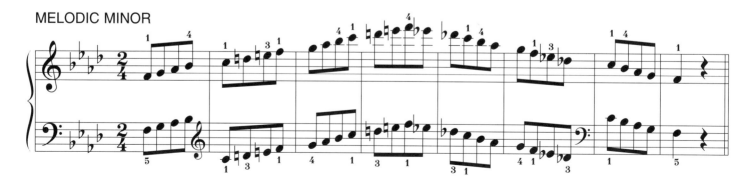

TRIADS and INVERSIONS — Block

DIMINISHED 7th — Block

TRIADS and INVERSIONS — Broken

ARPEGGIO — Root Position

1st Inversion

2nd Inversion

DIMINISHED 7th ARPEGGIO

CADENCE CHORDS

B♭ Minor
(RELATIVE OF D♭ MAJOR)

R.H. 4 on B♭

L.H. 4 on G or G♭

NATURAL MINOR — Quarters, 1 octave

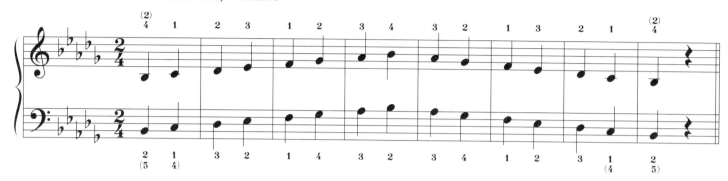

NATURAL MINOR — Eighths, 2 octaves

HARMONIC MINOR — Parallel motion

HARMONIC MINOR — Contrary motion

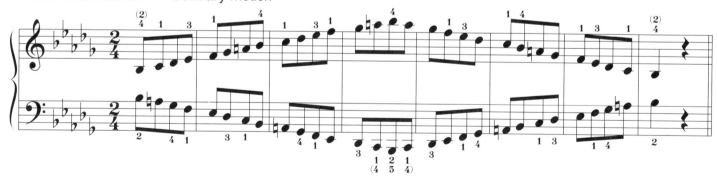

MELODIC MINOR

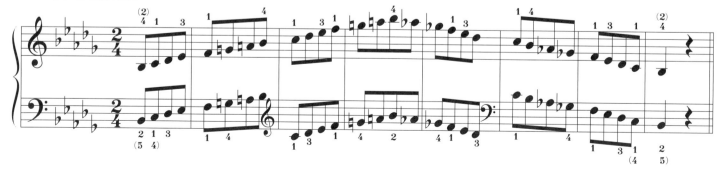

TRIADS and INVERSIONS — Block

DIMINISHED 7th — Block

TRIADS and INVERSIONS — Broken

ARPEGGIO — Root Position

1st Inversion

2nd Inversion

DIMINISHED 7th ARPEGGIO

CADENCE CHORDS

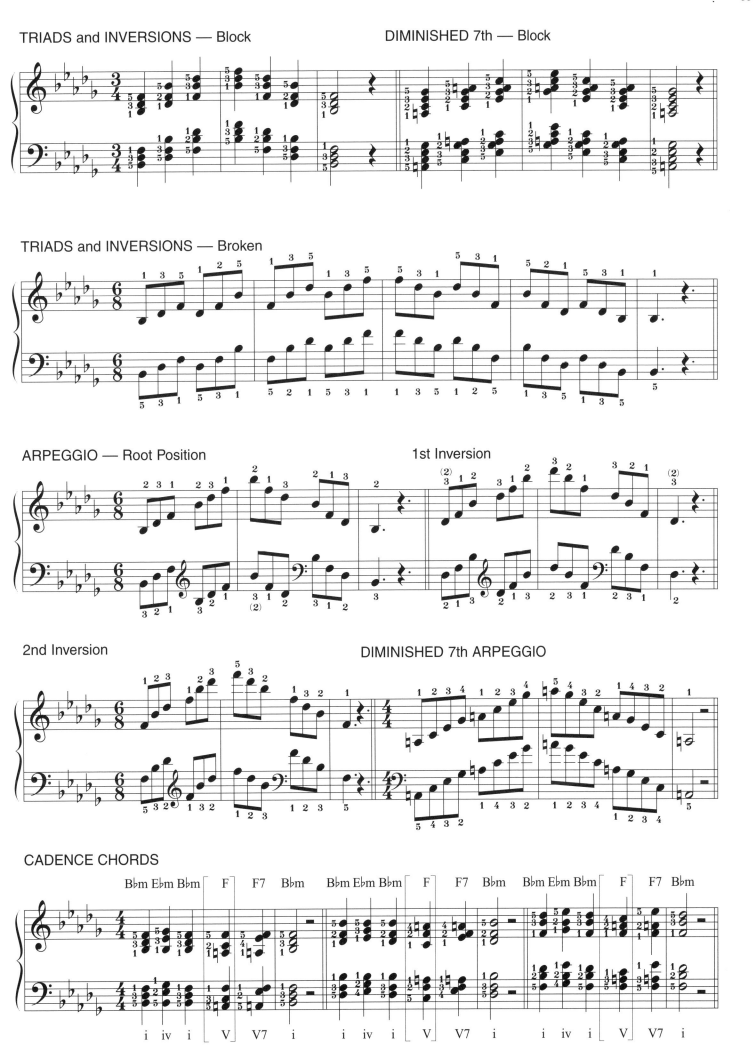

FJH1132

E♭ Minor
(RELATIVE OF G♭ MAJOR)

R.H. 4 on B♭

L.H. 4 on G♭

NATURAL MINOR — Quarters, 1 octave

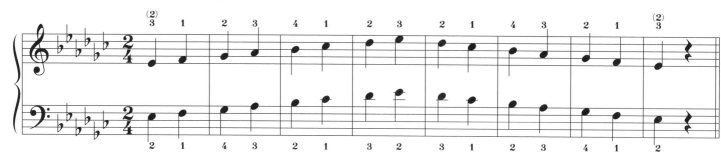

NATURAL MINOR — Eighths, 2 octaves

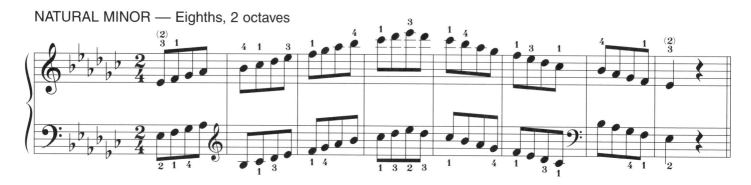

HARMONIC MINOR — Parallel motion

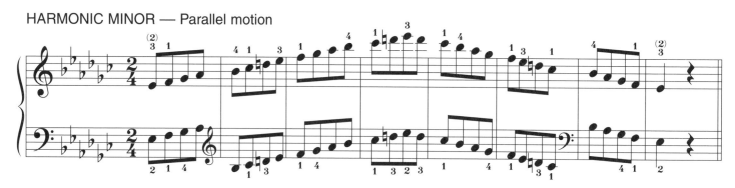

HARMONIC MINOR — Contrary motion

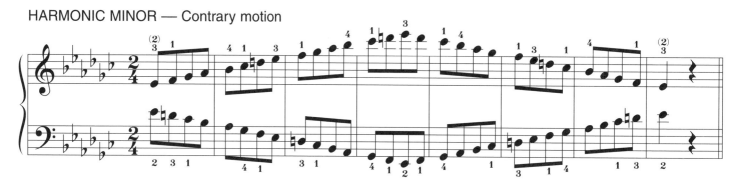

MELODIC MINOR

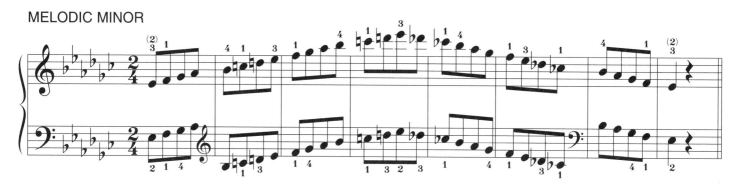

TRIADS and INVERSIONS — Block

DIMINISHED 7th — Block

TRIADS and INVERSIONS — Broken

ARPEGGIO — Root Position

1st Inversion

2nd Inversion

DIMINISHED 7th ARPEGGIO

CADENCE CHORDS

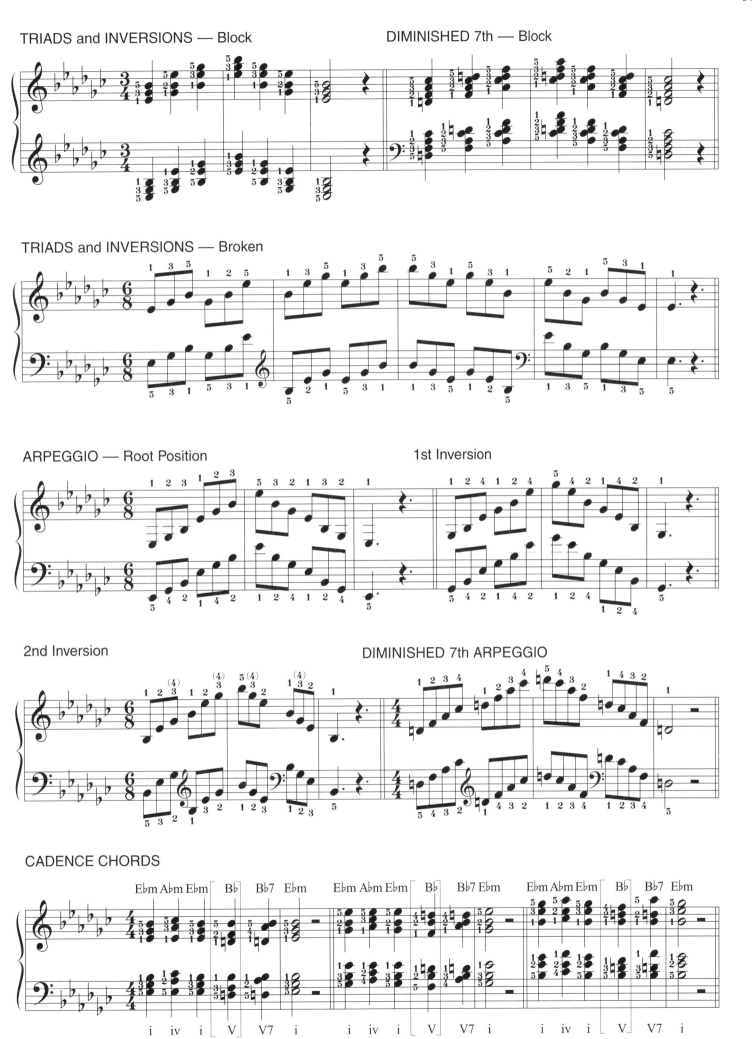

58

The Chromatic Scale

1. STANDARD FINGERING

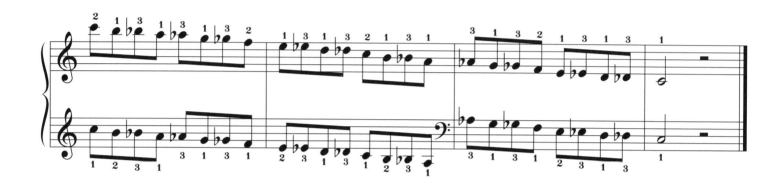

2. ALTERNATE FINGERING

The fingering below is useful for extended chromatic passages.
When playing more than two octaves, the fingering pattern repeats. Note that the thumbs play on every other white key.

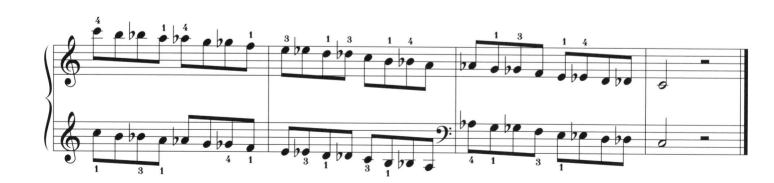

Pentatonic Scales

A pentatonic scale has only five notes. (*Penta* means five.)
Compared to the C major scale, the 4th and 7th notes are omitted:

C PENTATONIC

Pentatonic scales may also be built by using the black keys of the piano.
Each pattern is different, depending upon which black key begins the scale:

C♯ PATTERN

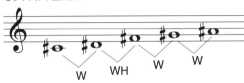

G♯ PATTERN

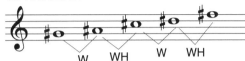

D♯ PATTERN

A♯ PATTERN

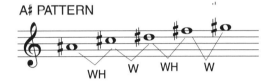

F♯ PATTERN

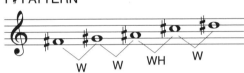

W	= 1 whole step
WH	= 1 whole step plus 1 half step

These scales may also be spelled using flats. In addition, they may also be transposed, starting on any note on the piano (including the white keys).

Pentatonic scales are common in folk music; in particular, the music of Asia, Europe, Scotland, Ireland, and Africa, as well as Native-American music. The French Impressionist composers, notably Claude Debussy and Maurice Ravel, often used these scales. (For example, see *Jimbo's Lullaby* and *Serenade for the Doll* from Debussy's *Children's Corner.*)

Whole-Tone Scales

A whole-tone scale is built using only whole steps. There are only two different whole-tone scales:

①

②

To build "new" whole-tone scales, begin on any note of either of the two scales above:

The French Impressionists frequently used the whole-tone scale to construct chords and for coloristic effects. (For example, see Debussy's *Voiles* from *Préludes, Book 1.*)
The whole-tone scale also occurs in jazz, especially in combination with the dominant seventh ♯5 chord.

Quick Guide to Scale Fingerings

Scale	Fingering	
Major — C, G, D, A, E minor — a, e, d, g, c	R.H. 12312345 L.H. 54321321	
B Major b minor	R.H. 12312345 L.H. 43214321	
F♯ (G♭) Major	R.H. 23412312 L.H. 43213214	
F Major f minor	R.H. 12341234 L.H. 54321321	
B♭ Major	R.H. 41231234 L.H. 32143213	
E♭ Major	R.H. 31234123 L.H. 32143213	
A♭ Major	R.H. 34123123 L.H. 32143213	
D♭ (C♯) Major	R.H. 23123412 L.H. 32143213	
f♯ minor	R.H. 34123123 L.H. 43213214	R.H. **ascending** melodic 34123412
c♯ minor	R.H. 34123123 L.H. 32143213	R.H. **ascending** melodic 34123412
g♯ minor	R.H. 34123123 L.H. 32143213	L.H. **descending** melodic 34123123
d♯ (e♭) minor	R.H. 31234123 L.H. 21432132	
b♭ (a♯) minor	R.H. 41231234 L.H. 21321432	

Rules Regarding Use of the 4th Finger:

The 4th finger only plays once in each octave, except for B and F major and minor.
The 4th finger of the R.H. plays B♭ if there is a B♭ in the scale, except for D and G minor.